MANCHESTER CITY FOOTBALL CLUB:
An A-Z

Dean Hayes

Published by Sigma Leisure – an imprint of
Sigma Press, 1 South Oak Lane, Wilmslow, Cheshire SK9 6AR, England.

British Library Cataloguing in Publication Data
A CIP record for this book is available from the British Library.

ISBN: 1-85058-552-0

Typesetting and Design by: Sigma Press, Wilmslow, Cheshire.

Printed by: MFP Design & Print

Cover Design: The Agency, Wilmslow

Photographs: EMPICS and Manchester City Football Club, except where stated

Contents

T h e   A - Z

ABANDONED MATCHES

An abandoned match may be defined as one which is called off by the referee while it is in progress, because conditions do not permit it to be completed. Generally speaking, far fewer matches are abandoned in modern times because if there is some doubt about the ability to play the full game, the match is more likely to be postponed.

On 11th January 1913, the Hyde Road ground was the venue for the FA Cup second round match with Sunderland. Official figures gave the attendance as 41,709 but some sources claim there were 50,000 inside the ground and a further 15,000 outside. As people spilled out on to the pitch as a result of the cramming, the referee had to abandon the game during extra-time with the score 0-0. The FA fined City £500 and Sunderland won the replay 2-0 some 25 days later. On 28th January 1961, Denis Law scored all six Manchester City goals in their fourth round FA Cup match at Luton Town. But, at 6-2 in City's favour, the referee abandoned the tie. City lost the replayed game 3-1, with Law scoring for them! Below is a list of abandoned League and Cup matches involving City:

Date	Opponents	Competition	Venue	Score
14.12.1895	Burslem Port Vale	Division 2	Home	1-0
21.12.1895	Burslem Port Vale	Division 2	Away	0-0
31.12.1898	Grimsby Town	Division 2	Away	0-0
21.12.1901	Stoke City	Division 1	Away	0-2
25.01.1902	Preston North End	FA Cup Rd 1	Away	1-1
25.10.1902	Barnsley	Division 2	Home	5-0
10.01.1903	Small Heath	Division 2	Home	0-0
11.01.1913	Sunderland	FA Cup Rd 2	Home	0-0
09.02.1921	Everton	Division 1	Home	0-0
28.11.1936	Brentford	Division 1	Home	0-0
07.01.1956	Blackpool	FA Cup Rd 3	Home	1-1
15.02.1958	Birmingham City	Division 1	Home	1-1
27.08.1960	Manchester United	Division 1	Home	2-2
28.01.1961	Luton Town	FA Cup Rd 4	Away	6-2
22.12.1962	Aston Villa	Division 1	Away	1-0
09.09.1965	Norwich City	Division 2	Home	1-1
01.02.1969	Newcastle United	Division 1	Home	1-1
22.02.1995	Ipswich Town	Premier	Home	2-0

AGE

Youngest

The youngest player to appear in a Football League fixture for Manchester City is Glyn Pardoe who made his league debut in the match against Birmingham City (Home 1-4) on 11th April 1962 when he was just 15 years 314 days old.

Oldest

The oldest player to line up in a City first team is Billy Meredith. He was 49 years 245 days old when he last turned out for the club against Newcastle United in an FA Cup semi-final on 29th March 1924. He was also the oldest player to play in a home international, when at almost 46 he played for Wales v England on 15th March 1920.

ALLISON, MALCOLM

Malcolm Allison's coaching and management days have often over-shadowed the fact that he was a fine centre-half in his playing days. His first club was Charlton Athletic for whom he signed in 1944 and later West Ham United. He played in 255 League and Cup games for the Hammers before being struck down with tuberculosis, which resulted in him losing a lung.

Allison took up his first management post with Bath City before Plymouth Argyle gave him his first job in League football.

In July 1965 he joined Joe Mercer at Maine Road to form one of the most successful partnerships in English football. One of the best coaches in the game, Allison was also one of the most explosive. In October of that year he was suspended for a month following a series of outbursts.

Yet Mercer and Allison revived the club. The Second Division championship was won in 1965-66. Two years later, the League title was gained and other trophies soon followed. City won the FA Cup in 1969 and the European Cup-Winners' Cup and Football League Cup the following year.

By 1972, Allison felt he deserved more than the tag of "assistant" and when Joe Mercer left for Coventry, he got his wish. Although after only nine months he left for Crystal Palace saying he could no longer motivate the City players. There followed another spell at Plymouth and periods coaching in Turkey and the United States before Allison returned to Maine Road in July 1979.

Malcolm Allison, 1967

After a number of disastrous million-pound signings, he lost his job and returned to Crystal Palace.

Thereafter, he took to travelling from one football outpost to another. Willington, a North-East non-league club was his first post, followed by spells in Kuwait and Portugal. In 1993 he was involved with Bristol Rovers but during his four months in charge as caretaker manager he was dogged by ill-health.

City fans meanwhile, prefer to remember the days when Allison worked with Joe Mercer to bring the good times back to Maine Road.

City's full League record under Malcolm Allison is:

P.	W.	D.	L.	F.	A.
83	23	25	35	96	137

AMATEURS

Only three amateurs have won FA Cup winners medals with professional sides since professionalism was legalised in 1885.

One of these was City's S.B. Ashworth when the Blues defeated Bolton Wanderers 1-0 in the 1904 FA Cup Final.

ANGLO-ITALIAN LEAGUE CUP

An annual match between the winners of the Football League Cup and Italian Cup. The League Cup winners were not guaranteed European football at the time, but once they gained automatic entry into the UEFA Cup in 1972, the competition ceased.

In September 1970, City played Bologna over two legs. Losing to the only goal of the game in Italy, City could only manage a 2-2 draw at Maine Road, with goals from Heslop and Lee and so lost 3-2 on aggregate.

ANGLO-SCOTTISH CUP

The Anglo-Scottish Cup was inaugurated in 1975-76 following the withdrawal of Texaco from the competition of that name. The qualifying stages took place during the pre-season on a league basis with the qualifying clubs going through to face Scottish opposition on a two-legged basis.

City only participated in that initial season, losing 1-0 at Blackpool and Blackburn before beating Sheffield United 3-1.

APPEARANCES

The players with the highest number of appearances for Manchester City FC are as follows:

	F. Lg	FA/FLg/Eur Cups	Total
Alan Oakes	561 (3)	104	665 (4)
Joe Corrigan	476	116	592
Mike Doyle	441 (7)	110	551 (7)
Bert Trautmann	508	37	545
Eric Brook	453	41	494
Colin Bell	393 (1)	96 (2)	489 (3)
Tommy Booth	380 (2)	96 (2)	476 (4)
Mike Summerbee	355 (2)	86	441 (2)
Paul Power	358 (7)	78 (2)	436 (9)
Willie Donachie	347 (4)	74 (1)	421 (5)

Consecutive Appearances:

Only Frank Swift and Joe Fagan have ever made over one hundred consecutive League appearances for the club immediately following their debuts.

Frank Swift: 195 appearances

Debut 25th December 1933 v Derby County (Away 1-4)

Joe Fagan: 121 appearances

Debut 1st January 1947 v Fulham (Home 4-0)

Six players have made over one hundred consecutive appearances at any time during their careers with Manchester City:

Joe Corrigan: 198 appearances

From 8th November 1975 to 23rd August 1980.

Eric Brook: 163 appearances

From 9th November 1929 to 7th October 1933.

Steve Redmond: 134 appearances

From 20th April 1986 to 25th August 1990.

Eric Westwood: 121 appearances

From 23rd August 1947 to 10th April 1950.

Alex Williams: 102 appearances

From 19th March 1983 to 14th September 1985.

Billy Murphy: 101 appearances

From 13th November 1920 to 24th February 1923.

ARDWICK FC

It was during 1887 that the Gorton captain, a Scot named McKenzie happened across a piece of waste ground in Ardwick. He felt it would serve as an ideal venue for Gorton AFC's games. In moving, the club was renamed Ardwick FC.

The club's first professional was Jack Hodgetts who received five shillings a week in 1887 (25p) and by 1888-89, Ardwick's fixture list had grown to 46 matches. The opposition included local sides from the Manchester area, Heaton Park, Gorton Villa and Newton Heath.

Over 60 goals were scored and only eight games lost. The club's reputation was enhanced by some outstanding results in local cup competitions. Ardwick twice won the Manchester Cup, beating Newton Heath 1-0 in 1891 and they also reached the Lancashire Junior Cup Final.

The 1891-92 season saw Ardwick playing in the Alliance where they finished seventh out of a dozen clubs. The Manchester club were admitted to the Second Division of the Football League in 1892. The captain at this time was Dave Russell, who had played with Nottingham Forest and Preston. In their first league game, Ardwick thrashed Bootle 7-0 and finished the season in fifth place.

But financial problems set in during 1893-94 and the club was forced into bankruptcy. It was Joshua ,Parlby who was largely responsible for rebuilding the ailing Ardwick club and as a result of his intervention, the club restarted as Manchester City Football Club, a limited liability company.

ASHWORTH, DAVID

David Ashworth was one of the smallest ever managers, for he stood just five feet tall. He was well known for his bowler hat and waxed moustache. A first-class referee from Waterford in Ireland, his first managerial post was with Oldham Athletic. Within four years of him taking charge, he had guided the team from the Lancashire Combination to the First Division of the Football League.

During the close season of 1914, Ashworth resigned to join Stockport County. He took over as Liverpool manager in December 1919 and after twice finishing in fourth place, he took them to the First Division championship in 1921-22. He surprised everyone by leaving the league champions in February 1923 to return to Oldham, but in July 1924 he joined City.

In his first season with City, Ashworth saw them score 76 goals – equal top-scorers in Division One – but only finish tenth. The club had just moved to Maine Road and this restricted the amount of money he had to spend on new players. After a poor start to the 1925-26 season he was sacked in November 1925. The club was eventually relegated to Division Two but reached the FA Cup Final.

Ashworth later managed Walsall and in the early post-war years was a scout for Blackpool, where he died on 23rd March 1947 aged 79.

City's full League record under David Ashworth is:

P.	W.	D.	L.	F.	A.
58	20	13	25	116	117

ATTENDANCES AT MAINE ROAD

Attendance figures at home provide some interesting statistics:

Individual Matches: Highest in the Football League

Opponents	Date	Competition	Attendance
Arsenal	23.02.1935	Division 1	79,491
Manchester United	20.09.1947	Division 1	78,000
Arsenal	10.04.1937	Division 1	74,918
Manchester United	28.12.1957	Division 1	70,483
Aston Villa	26.12.1929	Division 1	70,000
Wolverhampton Wands	23.08.1947	Division 1	67,800
Burnley	10.05.1947	Division 2	67,672
Burnley	02.05.1960	Division 1	65,981
Manchester United	09.01.1937	Division 1	64,862
Manchester United	11.09.1948	Division 1	64,502

Lowest Attendances (since the First World War)

Nottingham Forest	13.02.1924	Division 1	3,000
Sheffield United	04.11.1925	Division 1	7,000
Swindon Town	16.01.1965	Division 2	8,015
Middlesbrough	17.03.1964	Division 2	8,053

Other games at Maine Road

Stoke City	03.03.1934	FA Cup Rd 6	84,569
Cardiff City	08.03.1924	FA Cup Rd 4	76,166
Everton	03.03.1956	FA Cup Rd 6	76,129
Huddersfield Town	30.01.1926	FA Cup Rd 4	74,789
Manchester United	29.01.1955	FA Cup Rd 4	74,723
Stoke City	18.02.1928	FA Cup Rd 5	73,668
Bury	22.01.1938	FA Cup Rd 4	71,937
Liverpool	18.02.1956	FA Cup Rd 5	70,640
Bolton Wanderers	18.02.1933	FA Cup Rd 5	69,920
Sheffield Wednesday	21.02.1934	FA Cup Rd 5 (R)	68,614

Manchester City's average home attendances over the last ten years have been as follows:

1985-86	24,171	1990-91	27,874
1986-87	21,922	1991-92	27,690
1987-88	19,017	1992-93	24,698
1988-89	23,500	1993-94	26,709
1989-90	27,975	1994-95	22,744

AWAY

Best Away Wins

Opponents	Date	Competition	Score
Tranmere Rovers	26.12.1938	Division 2	9-3
Reading	31.01.1968	FA Cup Rd 3 (R)	7-0
Derby County	29.01.1938	Division 1	7-1
Wolverhampton Wands	21.03.1904	Division 1	6-1
Manchester United	23.01.1926	Division 1	6-1
Clapton Orient	06.03.1926	FA Cup Rd 6	6-1
Everton	15.09.1928	Division 1	6-2
Brentford	03.04.1937	Division 1	6-2
Plymouth Argyle	12.10.1988	FLg Cup Rd 2	6-3

Worst Away Defeats

Small Heath	17.03.1894	Division 2	2-10
Everton	03.09.1906	Division 1	1-9
West Brom Albion	21.09.1957	Division 1	2-9
Burton Wanderers	26.12.1894	Division 2	0-8
Wolverhampton Wands	23.12.1933	Division 1	0-8
Wolverhampton Wands	18.08.1962	Division 1	1-8
Sheffield United	26.10.1925	Division 1	3-8
Leicester City	22.02.1958	Division 1	4-8

Highest Scoring Away Draw:

Chelsea	03.02.1937	Division 1	4-4

Most away wins in a season	11 in 1988-89 (Division 2)
Fewest away wins in a season	0 in 1986-87 (Division 1)
Most away defeats in a season	16 in 1958-59 (Division 1)

Fewest away defeats in a season	4 in 1898-99 (Division 2) and 1902-03 (Division 2)
Most away goals in a season	51 in 1936-37 (Division 1)
Fewest away goals in a season	8 in 1986-87 (Division 1)

BALL, ALAN

Alan Ball played a major role in England's 1966 World Cup triumph. His tremendous work-rate was an inspiration for his team-mates and he went on to win 72 caps. His transfers broke the British record twice; when he moved from Blackpool to Everton in 1966, he cost £110,000 and when he moved from Everton to Arsenal in 1971, he cost a new record £220,000 fee.

He gained a League championship medal with Everton in 1969-70 and ended on the losing side in two FA Cup Finals. After further spells with Southampton, Blackpool and Bristol Rovers, he retired in 1984 with 743 League appearances under his belt.

Alan Ball

In May that year he took over as manager of Portsmouth and steered them into the First Division. Unfortunately, Pompey were relegated straight back the following season.

With Portsmouth struggling he was sacked in January 1989. After a short spell as Jock Wallace's assistant at Colchester, he moved to Stoke in a similar capacity to Mick Mills. Within two weeks he was made caretaker manager when the man who appointed him was fired. Later appointed manager, he lost his job in February 1991 with Stoke languishing in mid-table in the Third Division. Appointed manager of Exeter in August 1991 he moved to Southampton before becoming City's manager in July 1995.

BANANAS

In 1988-89 City's supporters became the country's pace-setters when they took large inflatable bananas to matches. When City entertained Leicester in the FA Cup that season even the players ran out with inflatable bananas!

It is difficult to trace the origins of the Craze, though the "Blue Print" fanzine may have had something to do with it, but it seemed to do the trick as City gained promotion at the end of the season.

BARKAS, SAM

Born at Tyne Dock, South Shields, Sam Barkas was a brilliant left-back who cost Manchester City £5,000 when signed from Third Division Bradford City in 1934. A most consistent and reliable defender, he always used the ball constructively when playing it out of defence. He was one of four brothers who played football at League level. He was an important member of City's 1936-37 League Championship winning team, figuring in defence alongside Bill Dale and Alex Herd. Though he only scored one goal in his 195 appearances for City, the winner against West Brom on the opening day of the 1934-35 season, it was his effective goal prevention that endeared him to the Maine Road faithful.

He was still fit enough at the age of 38 to captain City to the Second Division championship of 1946-47.

There is no doubt that he would have won more than his five England caps but for the presence of Arsenal's Eddie Hapgood on the international scene. Barkas left Maine Road after the end of the 1946-47 season to become manager of Workington Town. He returned to the North-west for a short spell in charge of Wigan Athletic before returning as a talent scout to his beloved Maine Road in 1957. His achievements for the club are commemorated by a bar named after, him in City's main stand.

BARNES, HORACE

Born at Wadsley Bridge near Sheffield, Horace Barnes' first league club was Derby County from whom he signed for Manchester City in 1914 for £2, 500. His career in wartime football saw him score 56 goals in 57 League games for City and incur a fine from the Manchester magistrates when he absented himself from working in a munitions factory to play against Stockport County in 1915.

Barnes forged a fine scoring partnership with Tommy Browell and had the distinction of scoring City's first goal at Maine Road against Sheffield United on 25th August 1923.

Horace Barnes had a fierce left foot shot and altogether scored 108 goals in 192 League games for City after the First World War – two of them against Liverpool on 27th March 1920 in front of King George V. Two of his goals also helped put an end to Burnley's record-breaking run of 30 games without defeat.

He played for England against Wales in a Victory international in 1919 and appeared twice for the Football League in 1921-22. When he moved to Preston North End in November 1924, City's fortunes began to fade as he and Tommy Browell were parted. In the twilight of his career, he proved that he had not lost his goal-scoring skill as he scored six goals in the first 30 minutes when playing for the Rest of Cheshire against Port Vale.

BELL, COLIN

Colin Bell began his career with Horden Colliery Welfare, where his potential was spotted by Bury. He made his league debut for the Shakers against Manchester City in February 1964, shortly before his 18th birthday. The following season he was Bury's leading goal-scorer and in March 1966 after scoring 25 goals in 82 games for the Shakers he signed for City for the very reasonable fee of £45,000.

He made his debut for City just three days after putting pen to paper against Derby County on 19th March. It was the season that Manchester City won promotion to the First Division after winning the Second Division championship. Bell played in the last 11 matches, scoring four goals, including one in his debut match. The following season

Colin Bell, 1971

with City back in the top flight, he ended as the club's top scorer with 12 goals, including a hat-trick against Stoke City. Glory followed with the FA Cup in 1969 and the League Cup and European Cup-Winners' Cup double in 1970.

He made his England debut in 1968 but it wasn't until after the 1970 World Cup that he began to establish himself in Sir Alf Ramsey's team. His non-stop running and enduring commitment in that infamous World Cup qualifying tie against Poland at Wembley wasn't enough to earn England a place in the finals. In total he made 48 England appearances and scored nine goals between 1968 and 1976. He is City's record-capped player and had it not been for a serious knee injury he would have featured in many more.

Bell had been signed for City by Joe Mercer, but in 1972 when Mercer left to become general manager at Coventry, Malcolm Allison who had been coach at Maine Road since 1965 took over. Allison said of Colin Bell: "At first he didn't seem to grasp his own freakish strength. He was the best, the most powerful runner in the business. "For a midfield player whose prodigious running was his prime quality, he was also an outstanding finisher and on 10th September 1974, he hit his second hat-trick for City as they beat Scunthorpe United 6-0 in a League Cup tie. On 12th November a tragedy struck as Bell was stretchered off in a fourth round League Cup tie against Manchester United following a challenge by Martin Buchan. He struggled to regain fitness, but pushed himself to the limit and beyond and was regularly seen running through the streets around Maine Road testing his knee.

He did make it back into the City side. On Boxing Day 1977, he came on as substitute against Newcastle United to one of the greatest ovations ever at Maine Road. He was not the player he had been two years earlier, though there was a time for one further honour, a Central League championship medal in 1977-78 before the injury forced him to retire in August 1979.

A model professional, Bell's balance and athleticism earned him the nickname "Nijinsky" after the racehorse. Now City's Youth Development Officer, there are few more popular figures at Manchester City than Colin Bell.

BENSON, JOHN

A colourful personality with a strong sense of humour off the field and a sense of duty on it, he joined Manchester City as an amateur in 1958 before turning professional three years later. After making 44 appearances, he moved to Torquay United and later Bournemouth, where he was made skipper by John Bond. In fact, he seemed to spend most of his career following Bond about. He played alongside him at Torquay, played under him at Bournemouth and Norwich City and coached under him at Manchester City and Burnley.

Taking over from Bond at Maine Road, he became manager in February 1983, something that he could never have thought possible when City let him go in June 1964. Probably a better coach than manager, he did not survive long after Luton won at Maine Road on the last day of the season to send City into the Second Division.

City's full League record under John Benson is:

P.	W.	D.	L.	F.	A.
17	3	2	12	13	32

BEST STARTS

Manchester City's best start to a Football League season came in 1914-15 when the club were unbeaten for the first eleven games of that campaign. Starting the season with a 4-1 home win over Bradford City with goals from Taylor, Howard, Barnes and Dorsett, the Blues went on to record the following best start:

P.	W.	D.	L.	F.	A.
11	7	4	0	17	6

BOND, JOHN

John Bond made his name as an outspoken manager after a career as a full-back for West Ham United and Torquay United. At Upton Park he developed into a steady, skilful defender who could read the game well and was a dead-ball expert, especially from the penalty spot. He scored eight goals in the Hammers' Second Division championship side of 1958-59 and also played in the club's 1964 FA Cup Final victory over Preston. At Torquay he helped them to promotion to Division Three before his retirement in 1969.

He went into management first with Bournemouth, then Norwich City, winning success for both clubs.

In October 1980, John Bond accepted an offer to join Manchester City, replacing Malcolm Allison and Tony Book after City had made a dreadful start to the season. He made three major signings, Tommy Hutchinson, Bobby McDonald and Gerry Gow. After losing to Birmingham in mid-October, they won ten of their next 15 League games and ended the season in 12th place. They also reached the League Cup semi-finals and the FA Cup Final, where they lost to Spurs in a replay. Bond also paid £1. 2 million for Trevor Francis in August 1981 but after looking championship contenders before Christmas, they finished tenth.

At the start of the 1982-83 season, Bond and his assistant Benson refused offers to work for Benfica, but after a good start, City began to falter and after a 4-0 FA Cup defeat at Brighton in February 1983, Bond resigned.

Since then he has managed Burnley, Swansea and Birmingham. Always attracting the attention of the media, he was fined by the

John Bond, 1982

FA in 1987 for allegedly bringing the game into disrepute following some unflattering remarks about the England coaching scene. In January 1990 he was appointed manager of Shrewsbury Town, but he resigned at the end of the 1992-93 season after they failed to make the Third Division play-offs after losing the last game of the season to relegation-threatened Northampton 3-2 after having being two goals up.

City's full league record under John Bond is:

P.	W.	D.	L.	F.	A.
98	39	26	33	128	

BOOK, TONY

A latecomer to full-time football, Tony Book did not kick his first ball in League soccer until just before his 29th birthday. It was Malcolm Allison who discovered Book when he was the manager of Southern League Bath City. When Allison moved to Plymouth Argyle, he took Book with him. Book missed only three games in two seasons at Home Park, where he became a great success.

Tony Book, 1967

Allison, now Joe Mercer's assistant at Maine Road, persuaded his boss to sign Book for £17,000. He missed only one League game in his first two seasons with City before his career looked to be over following an Achilles tendon injury late in 1968. However, upon his return, City had a great cup run which ended when they beat Leicester at Wembley in the 1969 FA Cup Final.

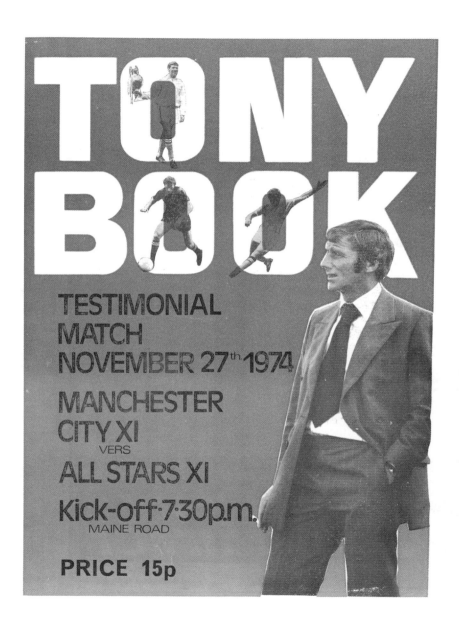

Book was voted Footballer of the Year with Derby's Dave Mackay at the end of the season.

He was back at Wembley the following year, carrying off the Football League Cup and seven weeks later, the European Cup Winners' Cup as City beat Gornik Zabrze 2-1.

Book retired from playing in 1973 and joined City's coaching staff, He became assistant to Ron Saunders and when Saunders left in 1974, Book took over as City manager. He soon found some success as a manager when City won the Football League Cup in 1976 and were runners-up in the League in 1976-77. In the summer of 1979, Book was made general manager with Allison returning as team manager and he later had an important behind-the-scenes role. Working with the younger players, he found some outstanding youngsters to win the FA Youth Cup for the first time in 1986. In November 1989 he was appointed caretaker-manager after Mel Machin was sacked and became first-team coach under Peter Reid in the 1990s.

City's full League record under Tony Book is:

P.	W.	D.	L.	F.	A.
210	88	60	62	310	246

BOOTH, TOMMY

Tommy Booth, 1972

Hailing from the Middleton estate of Langley, Tommy Booth had something of a meteoric rise to fame. Making his League debut in the 1-1 draw with Arsenal at Maine Road on 9th October 1968, he ended his first season by scoring the winning goal in the FA Cup semi-final against Everton at Villa Park. He also won an England Under-23 cap in that 1968-69 season and was once described by City manager Joe Mercer, as being like 'Stan Cullis and Neil Franklin rolled into one.'

He was City's first-choice centre-half for seven seasons, but lost his place when Dave Watson joined the Blues from Sunderland for £275,000. But Tommy Booth was a versatile player and when Colin Bell was injured, he moved into midfield and produced some very effective performances.

In his City career, Tommy Booth won several honours – FA Cup winners' medal, European Cup-winners' Cup medal and two League Cup winners' medals as well as playing in a third League Cup Final when City went down 2-1 to Wolves. After appearing in 480 first team games for City and scoring 34 goals, he was allowed to move to Preston North End in September 1981 for £30,000.

BOOTLE

Founder members of the Second Division in 1892-93 they resigned after just one season despite finishing eighth in the table, in fact, they were City's opponents on the opening day of the season, but were well-beaten 7-0 with Davies grabbing a hat-trick. They did gain revenge in the return fixture on Merseyside, winning 5-3.

BRADFORD PARK AVENUE

Park Avenue enjoyed 47 seasons in the League before failing to hold on to their place in 1969-70 after three consecutive seasons at the bottom of the league. They started their career in the Second Division in 1908-09, though it was a further five seasons before the two clubs first met – Bradford winning 3-1 at home and 3-2 at Hyde Road. The last season the two clubs met was 1946-47 when an Andy Black hat-trick helped City to a 7-2 victory at Maine Road.

BROOK, ERIC

Eric Brook began his career with Barnsley and in his first full season, 1926-27, he appeared in every League game scoring eleven goals. During that season, Fred Tilson joined the Oakwell club and they immediately became friends. On 14th March 1928, Fred joined Manchester City and although Eric was upset the partnership was to break up, the disappointment did not last, as just two days later he joined him at Maine Road, City paid Barnsley a combined fee of £6,000.

At the end of the season City won the Second Division championship, although Brook did not get a medal as he was just one game short of the required number of appearances.

In October 1929, he gained his first international cap as England defeated Northern Ireland 3-0 in Belfast. Unfortunately, that was his last international until May 1933 when he helped England defeat Switzerland 4-0 in Berne. He had by now established himself as City's regular outside-left. The 5ft 6ins fair-haired forward was unorthodox in his style and seemed to roam the forward line, popping up everywhere during a game.

The 1932-33 season saw City reach the FA Cup Final for the first time since 1926, with Brook scoring six goals during the cup run. He was very popular, both with supporters and team-mates due to his versatility, Brook once deputised at left-back before a full house at Old Trafford: and he went into goal for part of games against Grimsby, Arsenal and Chelsea. In 1933-34 he featured in all four international games and scored in every one, including his first Wembley international, a 3-0 victory over Scotland.

Eric Brook

He helped Manchester City achieve promotion, win the FA Cup and in 1936-37, the League Championship, while at the same time score so many goals, that even today he remains the club's leading goalscorer with 178 goals (159 in the League). His playing career came to an end not long after the outbreak of war. He and City left-back Sam Barkas, were involved in a car crash on the way to a game and although Barkas went on to play for a number of years after the accident, Eric Brook's career was over at the age of 32.

BROTHERS

There have been a number of instances of sets of brothers playing for Manchester City.

Albert and Peter, Fairclough both signed on the same day from Eccles Borough in 1913 and both forwards left in the summer of 1920. George Dorsett joined Manchester City from West Bromwich Albion in December 1904 for a then record fee of £450 for a winger. City switched him to wing-half and he went on to make 211 first-team appearances scoring 65 goals. In 1910 he was joined by his brother Joe who was also an outside-left with West Brom. The two played together for a total of 16 matches.

Paul and Ron Futcher were the only set of twins to play for City, both joining the club from Luton Town in 1978. Darren and Jason Beckford both appeared in City's teams of the late 1980s, though never in the same side.

Ian and David Brightwell are the latest set of brothers to play for City. David is a promising central defender and younger brother of the more experienced full-back, Ian.

BROWELL, TOM

Hull City were so eager to sign Tom Browell that in 1910 two of the club's directors rowed across the River Tyne to reach the colliery village of walbottle where he lived. In October of that year, 18-year-old Browell hit a hat-trick against Stockport County and after one journalist had written that "ten men and a boy beat Stockport", Browell became known as "Boy" Browell.

His scoring feats for the Tigers attracted the bigger clubs and in December 1911, Everton paid £1,650 for him. In just 17 games that season, Browell scored 12 goals and almost helped the Goodison Park club to the title. In October 1913 City paid £1,780 for Browell's services. He went on to forge a deadly attacking partnership with Horace Barnes that was to terrify opposition defences. He made his debut for the Maine Road club on 8th November scoring in a 2-1 home defeat by Sheffield Wednesday. He top-scored for City in four seasons with a best of 31 in 1920-21 and had a total of 122 League goals in

222 games. In his final season with the club he scored all four goals in a 4-4 draw with Everton at Maine Road and five goals in the 8-3 win over Burnley, His effort in the 1926 FA Cup Final against Bolton Wanderers almost rescued City when only a brilliant save from Dick Pym denied him. Browell was transferred to Blackpool for £1,500 in September 1926 and at the age of 37 was still playing for the Seasiders some four years later.

BURTON SWIFTS

One of the founder members of the Second Division, honours were even of the fourteen matches played between the two sides. City's biggest win in this fixture was 9-0 in the final game of the 1897-98 season with Meredith and Whitehead both grabbing hat-tricks.

BURTON UNITED

One of the founder members of the Second Division as Burton Swifts in 1892, they merged with Burton Wanderers (after they left the League) to form Burton United. City played them in 1902-03 winning both matches, 5-0 at home and 2-0 away. They failed to gain re-election after finishing bottom of the Second Division in 1906-07.

BURTON WANDERERS

They spent three seasons in the Second Division between 1894 and 1897. After drawing at home 1-1, City travelled to Burton and were beaten 8-0 on Boxing Day 1894. The following season, Burton finished fourth and whilst the game at Hyde Road once again ended 1-1, the Wanderers beat the Blues 4-1. It was November 1896 before City won their one and only match against them, with F. Williams and J.Gunn scoring in a 2-1 victory.

CAPTAINS

One of the club's earliest captains, Billy Meredith received the FA Cup from Lord Alfred Lyttleton following City's 1-0 defeat of Bolton Wanderers at The Crystal Palace.

Max Woosnam was City skipper when they entertained Sheffield United on the opening day of the new Maine Road stadium. An all-round sportsman, he was a member of Britain's Davis Cup team and gained a Cambridge Blue at soccer, golf and lawn tennis. A Wimbledon doubles champion, he gained an Olympic gold medal at tennis. Sam Cowan played in three FA Cup Finals with a winners' medal in 1934 when he collected the trophy as captain of the side, Sam Barkas was 38 when he captained City to the Second Division championship in 1946-47.

Roy Paul captained Manchester City to success in the 1956 FA Cup Final, twelve months after he had collected a losers' medal against Newcastle United.

Tony Book's influence as captain of Manchester City was enormous, leading the club to victory in the FA Cup, European Cup-winners' Cup, Football League Cup and to the Second Division championship.

Captain of the City Youth Cup-winning team of 1986, Steve Redmond became the club's youngest-ever skipper when he succeeded Kenny Clements as City captain in 1988. The following season he graduated to the captaincy of the England Under-21 team.

CENTRAL LEAGUE

The Central League originated in 1911 to serve primarily the clubs in the North and Midlands reserve teams. Manchester City came close on a number of occasions to winning the Central League championship but had to wait until 1977-78 for that honour. They won the title again in 1986-87. The club's record in those two seasons was as follows:

	P.	W.	D.	L.	F.	A.	Pts
1977-1978	42	27	8	7	92	40	62
1986-1987	34	23	4	7	83	46	73

In 1931-32, City scored 106 goals – the only time they achieved this feat in the Central League.

CENTURIES

Goals:

Manchester City have scored a century of goals in a Football League season on four occasions. The club scored 108 goals in 1926-27 when finishing third in Division Two and 100 goals the following season when winning the Second Division championship. They scored 107 goals in winning the First Division title in 1936-37 and 104 goals in 1957-58 to finish fifth in the First Division.

There are twelve instances of individual players who have scored a hundred or more goals for City in the League.

Eric Brook is the greatest goal-scorer with 159 strikes in his City career (1928-1940) while Tom Johnson scored 158 goals between 1919 and 1930. other century-scorers are Billy Meredith, 145; Joe Hayes, 142; Billy Gillespie, 126; Tom Browell, 122; Horace Barnes, 120; Colin Bell, 117; Frank Roberts, 116; Francis Lee, 112; Fred Tilson, 110; and Alex Herd, 107.

Appearances

Only Frank Swift and Joe Fagan have made over a hundred consecutive appearances immediately after making their Football League debuts.

CHAMPIONSHIPS

Manchester City have on eight occasions won a divisional championship.

1898-99 Division Two

Billy Meredith's contribution to Manchester City's success was outstanding as the Blues lost only five of their 34 league games in obtaining a club record 52 points. The Welshman top-scored with 29 goals from 33 games. During the course of the season the club enjoyed a thirteen-match unbeaten run in which eleven games were won and two drawn.

	P.	W.	D.	L.	F.	A.	Pts
Manchester City	34	23	6	5	92	35	52
Glossop North End	34	20	6	8	76	38	46
Leicester Fosse	34	18	9	7	64	42	45

1902-03 Division Two

Relegated the previous season, City were determined to bounce back to Division One immediately. This they did after losing only five and drawing four of their 34 matches. The Blues scored a league record of 95 goals of which Gillespie scored 30 and Meredith 22. There were some outstanding home performances as Gainsborough Trinity were beaten 9-0, Burslem Port Vale 7-1 and Burnley 6-0.

	P.	W.	D.	L.	F.	A.	Pts	
Manchester City	34	25	4	5	95	29	54	
Small Heath	34	24	3	7	74	36	51	Woolwich
Arsenal	34	20	8	6	66	30	48	

1909-10 Division Two

Relegated in 1908-09, the Blues soon shot back to the top flight, having lost only seven of their 38 league matches in Division Two. Two of these defeats came at the hands of neighbours Oldham Athletic who finished as runners-up to City. It was a season in which City scored 81 goals with Dorsett, Holford, Wynn, Thornley, Jones and Conlin all reaching double figures.

	P.	W.	D.	L.	F.	A.	Pts
Manchester City	38	23	8	7	81	40	54
Oldham Athletic	38	23	7	8	79	39	53
Hull City	38	23	7	8	80	46	53

1927-28 Division Two

After the disappointments of the previous season when five-thou-sandths of a goal kept City in Division Two, the Maine Road side completed the season two points ahead of Leeds United whom they had defeated home and away. Scoring 100 goals, City registered their fourth Second Division championship success in their last five seasons in that Division.

	P.	W.	D.	L.	F.	A.	Pts
Manchester City	42	25	9	8	100	59	59
Leeds United	42	25	7	10	98	49	57
Chelsea	42	23	8	11	75	45	54

1936-37 Division One

After losing the opening game of the season at Ayresome Park, City began their home matches in fine form, with two good wins, 4-0 against Leeds United and 6-2 against West Bromwich Albion. However, they then won only one of their next ten games. Following the return of City centre-forward Fred Tilson at the end of the year – he was injured in early September – the Blues began to move relentlessly up the table. The goals too began to flow with 20 being scored in six games. The biggest crowd of the season, 74,918, saw City beat Arsenal 2-0. On 24th April 1937, City faced Sheffield Wednesday in their last home game of the season, needing two points to clinch the League Championship. Eric Brook set them on their way to a 4-1 win to claim their first League Championship.

	P.	W.	D.	L.	F.	A.	Pts
Manchester City	42	22	13	7	107	61	57
Charlton Athletic	42	21	12	9	58	49	54
Arsenal	42	18	16	8	80	49	52

1946-47 Division Two

The Blues had been in Division Two since 1938 just a season after winning the First Division Championship for the first time. After enjoying a 3-0 win over Leicester City in the opening match they went on to lose only two of their first dozen league fixtures.

From 16th November 1946 to 19th April 1947, the Blues played 22 league games without defeat. The promotion battle ended in May when City defeated Burnley 1-0 in front of a Maine Road crowd of 67,672.

	P.	W.	D.	L.	F.	A.	Pts
Manchester City	42	26	10	6	78	35	62
Burnley	42	22	14	6	65	29	58
Birmingham City	42	25	5	12	74	33	55

1965-66 Division Two

Just before the start of this season, Joe Mercer invited Malcolm Allison to join the Maine Road staff. The chemistry seemed to work as City won the Division Two championship, losing only five out of 42 matches. Promotion was guaranteed when Colin Bell scored the only goal of the game at Rotherham on 4th May 1966.

	P.	W.	D.	L.	F.	A.	Pts
Manchester City	42	22	15	5	76	45	59
Southampton	42	22	10	10	85	56	54
Coventry City	42	20	13	9	73	53	53

1967-68 Division One

In the opening game on 19th August 1967, City drew with Liverpool before losing their next two matches. Following Francis Lee's debut on 14th October against Wolves, the Blues embarked on an 11-match unbeaten run and by Christmas were in a comfortable place in Division One. In fact, it was 23rd March before City lost their first match of 1968, 2-0 at Elland Road. There were memorable meetings with Manchester United as the two sides vied for the League Championship. The Reds won 2-1 at Maine Road in September but on 27th March, City won 3-1 at Old Trafford, despite going a goal down after just 35 seconds. The final game of the season saw City travel to Newcastle and in a thrilling encounter win 4-3 to bring the League Championship to Maine Road for the second time in the club's history.

	P.	W.	D.	L.	F.	A.	Pts
Manchester City	42	26	6	10	86	43	58
Manchester United	42	24	8	10	89	55	56
Liverpool	42	22	11	9	71	40	55

CHARITY SHIELD

Manchester City have appeared in the FA Charity Shield on seven occasions. The results have been as follows:

Date	Opponents	Venue	Score
28.11.1934	Arsenal	Highbury	0-4
04.11.1937	Sunderland	Maine Road	2-0
24.10.1956	Manchester United	Maine Road	1-0
03.08.1969	West Bromwich Albion	Maine Road	6-1
02.08.1970	Leeds United	Elland Road	1-2
05.08.1973	Aston Villa	Villa Park	1-0
18.08.1974	Burnley	Maine Road	0-1

CLARKE, ROY

Born in Newport, South Wales, Roy Clarke's first taste of international recognition was as a member of the Welsh Schools Baseball team in 1939. During the Second World War, he worked in the coal-mines, but managed to play football for a local side at the weekends. He later joined Cardiff City, for whom he made 39 appearances and scored 11 goals before joining Manchester City. Roy Clarke holds the unique record of playing in three different divisions of the Football League in three consecutive League games!

Roy Clarke

He played his last game for the Bluebirds, who were at the time Third Division champions in their penultimate game of the 1946-47 season before he joined the Maine Road club. He played in City's last game of their Second Division promotion winning season against his hometown club, Newport County – a game in which George Smith scored all five goals as City beat the Welsh side 5-1. Clarke's next game was at the start of the 1947-48 campaign with City in the top flight. They beat Wolves 4-3 at Molineux with Roy Clarke hitting the winner.

He won his first international cap for Wales against England in 1948 and his last eight years later against Northern Ireland. He made 22 appearances for his country, scoring 5 goals.

Clarke was a left-winger with a very powerful shot and scored many vital goals during his stay at Maine Road. He was instrumental in City getting to Wembley at the end of the 1954-55 campaign. He hit both goals in the 2-0 win at Kenilworth Road as City disposed of Luton Town in the fifth round. He also hit the only goal of the semi-final against Sunderland at Villa Park, but unfortunately Newcastle beat City in the Final 3-1.

The following season though, he did pick up an FA Cup winners' medal after City had beaten Birmingham 3-1. His best season for City was 1956-57 when he scored 11 goals from his 40 appearances.

In September 1958, he moved on to nearby Stockport County on a free transfer, where he played a further 25 league games for the Edgeley Park outfit. He had played in 349 League games for Manchester City and scored 73 goals.

He returned to Maine Road in 1966 to run the City Social Club. After twenty-two years, he retired on 27th September 1988, with hundreds of friends and colleagues paying tribute to him in a farewell party at Maine Road.

CLEAN SHEET

This is the colloquial expression to describe a goalkeeper's performance when he does not concede a goal.

In the Football League, Joe Corrigan kept twenty-two clean sheets in 42 appearances as City finished runners-up in the First Division in 1976-77 whilst Alex Williams kept twenty-one clean sheets from the same number of games as City finished third in Division Two to gain promotion on goal difference.

COLOURS

The first recorded strip in which City's forerunners, West Gorton St Marks played in was black with a silver Maltese cross on the front.

From then until the present day sky blue kit, Manchester City have worn a long procession of different coloured football kits.

In their early days, the City players had to make do with kits that looked more like pyjamas than sporting attire. Large loose "grandad" vests were worn with even bigger baggier "knickers" as they were called then!

Since City wore the maroon strip in the 1934 FA Cup Final win over Portsmouth, all the club's kits have been manufactured by the Wythenshawe-based company Umbro. They have over the last 61 years kitted the players out in a variety of colours – blue and white, red and black, purple and white, maroon and yellow! There is no doubt in most City followers minds that blue and white are the club's most evocative colours, but the Blue's luckiest colours are red and black. The vertically striped red and black outfit travelled with the club to the 1968 League Championship, the 1969 League Cup and the European Cup-Winners' Final in 1970.

CONSECUTIVE HOME GAMES

City have been involved in three intense sequences of five home games in succession on three occasions, but in 1923-24 and 1981-82 they included FA Cup ties. Between 24th January and 28th February 1903, City played five consecutive league games at Hyde Road and not only won them all, but scored 30 goals in the process. They ended the season as champions of Division Two.

Date	Opponents	Score
24.01.1903	Chesterfield	4-2
31.01.1903	Burnley	6-0
14.02.1903	Burslem Port Vale	7-1
23.02.1903	Small Heath	4-0
28.02.1903	Gainsborough Trinity	9-0

CORRIGAN, JOE

Joe Corrigan joined Manchester City as a junior in 1966 when he was playing for Sale Football Club. After being singled out in club trials where he gave some impressive performances, he turned professional

Joe Corrigan

at Maine Road in January 1967. His first-team debut for City was in the League Cup tie against Blackpool at Maine Road, which ended 1-1 in October of the same year. He had to wait until March 1969 for his Football League debut at Portman Road, Ipswich, beating City 2-1. In his early days he was always in the shadow of Harry Dowd and Ken Mulhearn, though when he did get a chance, he was inconsistent. Despite this unimpressive start to his League career, he fought hard to establish himself, but faced another crisis of confidence when in 1975, City signed Keith MacRae for £100,000 from Motherwell. Out of favour with the then City manager Ron Saunders, he asked for a transfer and was transfer-listed in February 1974. However, once again the 6ft 4ins goalkeeper buckled down and won back his first-team place, going on to serve City for a further nine years. Manchester City have had three outstanding goalkeepers since the war – Swift, Trautmann and Corrigan was the third. I'm sure if he'd been around at a different time than Ray Clemence and Peter Shilton, he would have collected far more than the nine caps he did win. He won his first in 1976, coming on as substitute against Italy in New York and his last against Iceland in 1982. He also played an unofficial international for England against Atletico Bilbao in 1981, plus ten appearances for England 'B'. His best season for City was 1976-77 when he only conceded 34 goals in his 42 appearances, keeping a record 22 clean sheets.

He won League Cup honours in 1970 and 1976 and a European Cup-Winners' Cup medal in 1970 when City beat Gornik Zabrze 2-1. When City played Tottenham Hotspur in the 1981 FA Cup Final, Corrigan had looked unbeatable – the game ending at 1-1. For his heroics between the posts, Corrigan was named man-of-the-match, though he was beaten three times in the replay, as the North London side won 3-2.

Corrigan played in 476 League games for Manchester City and in another 116 Cup matches, making him second only to Alan Oakes in terms of the number of first-team games for City.

In March 1983 City transferred him to Seattle Sounders in the NASL for £30,000. He later returned to these shores to play for Brighton, Norwich and Stoke City before retiring.

COWAN, SAM

The story is told that Sam Cowan did not kick a football until he was 17 when he took part in a local park game at the last minute and wearing only one borrowed boot!

A hefty pivot who was happiest in an attacking role, Sam Cowan was a resourceful and enthusiastic player. He once scored a hat-trick of headers for Doncaster Rovers against Halifax in March 1924. In December of that year, he joined Manchester City and in his 12 years with the club he captained them to three FA Cup Finals and won a Second Division championship medal in 1928-29.

His versatility showed when he won the first of his three England caps as a left-half. He also played for the Football League against the Irish League in 1934. Cowan scored 24 goals in 406 games for City.

In October 1935 he moved to Bradford City for £2,000 and later played for Mossley and was Brighton trainer before returning to Maine Road as manager in 1946. During his only season in charge he led the side to the Second Division championship. He continued to live in Hove and in June 1947, when the City directors expressed concern at his commuting, he decided to leave Maine Road and concentrate on his physiotherapy business in the Sussex town. He died in 1964 whilst refereeing a charity match in Hayward's Heath.

City's full League record under Sam Cowan is:

P.	W.	D.	L.	F.	A.
42	26	10	6	78	35

CRICKETERS

Manchester City have had two players who were also cricketers of real distinction. The first of these was E. H. "Patsy" Hendren.

Patsy Hendren, small, stocky, with a ready London wit, was loved by crowds and deeply respected by opposing bowlers as a master craftsman. Speaking once at a cricket dinner he accidentally knocked over his chair as he rose to speak and immediately quipped: "That's by no means the first time I've heard the sound of falling timber behind me." Hendren's career had begun as early as 1907 and he did not completely retire until 1938. Playing for England in 51 Tests, he

Sam Cowan

scored 40,302 runs for his county Middlesex at a batting average of 48.82. For City this powerful wing-forward only managed two games in the 1908-09 season.

Jack Dyson was an all-rounder for Lancashire between the years 1954-64. He scored 4,433 runs and captured 161 wickets. For City he played in 72 first-team games. He scored a goal in the 1956 FA Cup Final and twice broke a leg in 1957-58.

CROWD TROUBLE

However unwelcome, crowd disturbances are far from a modern phenomenon at major football matches and there is plenty of hooliganism and disorder at matches around the turn of the century.

One game between Lower Hurst and Ardwick was abandoned in 1889 because of crowd invasion and later the same season a match against West Manchester was abandoned because two players were fighting. On 11th January 1913 the Hyde Road ground was the venue for the FA Cup second round match with Sunderland. The official attendance was given as 41, 709 but sources claim there were 50,000 inside the ground. As people began to spill on to the pitch, the referee had to abandon the game.

In March 1993, a pitch invasion during the sixth round FA Cup tie with Tottenham Hotspur raised the debate about perimeter fences. However, behaviour at Maine Road has usually been of a high standard!

CURLE, KEITH

When Keith Curle joined Manchester City from Wimbledon in August 1991 for a hefty £2.5 milllion fee, he became the costliest defender in British football. He quickly assumed the role as City's skipper before graduating to the full England side. City's penalty taker, he remains a top-quality central-defender with great pace.

Keith Curle

DARWEN

Darwen joined the League when it was extended to 14 clubs in 1891-92 but finished bottom of the table and conceded 112 goals in 26 games. They joined City in the new Second Division the following season and won promotion at the first attempt, beating City 3-1 at home but going down 4-2 away. The two clubs last met in 1898-99 when City won 10-0 at home and 2-0 away; Darwen finishing bottom of the table and conceding a League record 141 goals. They failed to gain re-election.

DEATH

Di Jones was already an international star when he joined City from Bolton Wanderers at the start of the 1898-99 season. He was City captain when he met with a sad and most untimely death. In August 1902, he gashed his knee in a friendly game. Within a week the wound had turned septic and Jones, who had played in 118 games for City was dead.

DEBUTS

Fred Howard had a remarkable debut for City on 18th January 1913 when he scored all four goals in the club's 4-1 win over Liverpool. Jimmy Constantine also scored a hat-trick on his debut, hitting all three goals as City won at Millwall 3-0.

On 5th May 1976, Mick Docherty made his City debut against Manchester United at Old Trafford. The Reds who won the game 2-0 were managed by Tommy Docherty, Mick's father.

Howard White's league career with City was cruelly cut short in the early 1970s. Making his debut against Liverpool he had to leave the action with a broken ankle and never got another chance.

One of the most unusual debuts was that by James Conlin. He was one of several players who had to leave the field suffering from heat exhaustion when City finished with six men against Woolwich Arsenal on 1st September 1906.

DEFEATS

Individual Games:

City's worst home defeat in a first-class match was the 7-2 scoreline inflicted on the club by West Bromwich Albion on 1st January 1934. Away from Maine Road, the club's heaviest defeat has been 10-2 v Small Heath on 17th March 1894.

Over a Single Season:

City's worst defensive record in terms of defeats suffered in a single season was twenty-two in seasons 1958-59 and 1959-60. Conversely, City only lost five matches in 1965-66 when they won the Second Division title. They also only lost five matches in 1895-96, 1898-99 and 1902-03, though from fewer matches played.

Consecutive League matches without defeat:

City's best run of league games without defeat is twenty-two and was established on two occasions: 26th December 1936 (at home to Middlesbrough 2-1) to 28th August 1937 (away at Wolves 1-3) and from 16th November 1946 (at home to Coventry City 1-0) to 3rd May 1947 (at home to Newcastle United 0-2).

DEFENSIVE RECORDS

Manchester City's best defensive record in the Football League was established in 1902-03 when the club won the Second Division championship, following relegation the previous season, City conceded just twenty-nine goals from that 34-match campaign and were beaten in just five matches.

The club's worst defensive record in the Football League was in 1962-63 when they let in 102 goals in 42 matches and were relegated from Division One.

DISMISSALS

Although sendings-off are an all-too-common feature of the modern game, no-one should think that football has ever been immune from them.

Irvine Thornley was something of a controversial figure and in January 1912 whilst captaining City, was sent off at Aston Villa it was his first game back following a five-match absence with an eye injury.

Since the war, two City goalkeepers, Bert Trautmann and Eric Nixon have been sent off. In the Manchester derby of 1949, City's W. Linacre and United's Cockburn were dismissed as were Mike Doyle and Lou Macari in the derby of March 1974. In February 1973 City's Tony Towers was sent off against Sunderland after scoring the opening goal in a 2-2 draw in the fifth round of the FA Cup.

Niall Quinn holds the unenviable record of being the first player in the Premier League to be dismissed when he was sent off against Middlesbrough on 19th August 1992.

PETER DOHERTY

The mercurial flame-haired Irishman was one of the outstanding players of his generation, the complete inside-forward and a great crowd favourite.

Born at Coleraine in Northern Ireland, he was barely 15 when the local Irish League club watched him playing junior football for Station United and invited him for a trial, What happened that Saturday was a trailer for Doherty's whole turbulent career. The shy red-headed boy was hustled into the dressing room and told to put on a jersey because the right-winger had missed his train. He did not receive one pass throughout the first-half, nobody spoke to him at half-time and when the winger did eventually appear, the substitute was ordered to give up his shirt.

Doherty sold to Blackpool by Glentoran for £2,000 in 1933 was signed by City in February 1936. He had developed into an astonishing all-purpose forward. His speed, his stamina, his versatility, his ability both to score spectacular goals and help out his defence, were all remarkable.

Doherty was the star of the 1936-37 Championship side, scoring 30 goals in 41 games. He was also top-scorer with 23 the following relegation season and in all, scored 81 times in 133 games for City. A goal he hooked home against Arsenal at Maine Road, almost from the goal-line was characteristic of his feats of individual virtuosity.

At the same time, he found playing for Ireland a bitter experience turning up at the last moment to meet a crowd of virtual strangers, with no chance to work out tactics and barely the chance to get to know one another. After the war, he linked up with Raich Carter at Derby to help the Rams win the FA Cup in 1946, Later that year Doherty had the almost inevitable quarrel with Derby, who refused to let him open a pub and moved on to Huddersfield Town, then struggling at the foot of the First Division.

Northern Ireland had never employed a team manager when Doherty took them over in the late fifties and had certainly never even begun to generate the atmosphere of comradeship and dedication he achieved. Doherty died in Poulton-le-Fylde near Blackpool in April 1990.

DONACHIE, WILLIE

Born in Glasgow, Willie Donachie joined Manchester City as a junior

Willie Donachie

in 1968. In those days he was a midfield player but it was after City had converted him to a left-back that his career took off. He replaced the unfortunate Glyn Pardoe after that player had broken a leg and for the next seven years made the position his own. In the seventies, Donachie was one of the best full-backs in the First Division. He was a member of the Scotland team that beat England at Hampden in 1976 and two years later, played in the World Cup Finals, In fact, only Asa Hartford with 36, won more Scottish caps as a City player than Willie Donachie's 35.

He was an ever-present in 1973-74 and 1976-77 league campaigns and played for City in two Football League Cup Finals, picking up a winners' medal in 1976. In March 1980 after appearing in 426 first-team games for City, the classy defender signed for NASL club Portland Timbers for £200,000. Later he played for Norwich, Burnley and Oldham. He is now Joe Royle's right-hand man at Goodison Park.

DOYLE, MIKE

Mike Doyle was a very determined player in whatever position he was given. Born in Manchester, he played for Stockport Boys before joining the Maine Road ground staff in 1962. He made his first-team debut for Manchester City as a centre-forward against Cardiff City on 12th March 1965. after giving impressive displays for the Youth and Central League sides. He went on to make more than 500 first-team appearances for City in either midfield or defence. It was his influence during the 1965-66 season that went a long way in helping City get out of the Second Division. Certainly not a prolific goal-scorer, when

Mike Doyle

he did score they were usually important goals. He scored six goals in a four-match spell over the Christmas period that season to help consolidate City's position at the top of the division. He was also instrumental in City topping the First Division in 1968. It was during this season that he played in his first representative game playing for the England Under-23s against Hungary and for Young England against an England XI. There followed appearances for the Football League, the first in 1972 against the Scottish League. Doyle seemed to save his goals for the European competitions or for the domestic trophy finals.

He scored the equalising goal at Wembley in the 1970 League Cup Final after West Bromwich Albion had gone a goal up, City going on to lift the trophy after Glyn Pardoe had hit the winner. In April 1970, he scored one of the goals in the European Cup-Winners' Cup semi-final second leg against Schalke 04, City winning 5-1 after losing by the only goal in Germany.

The following month he had an outstanding first half against Gornik Zabrze in Vienna as City won their first European trophy. The Maine Road side had gone into half-time two goals ahead and though they conceded a goal in the 68th minute after Doyle had gone off with an injured ankle, they hung on. He also scored against the Polish side in the 1970-71 Cup-Winners' Cup campaign. Doyle scored to make it 2-2 on aggregate and force a third match which City won 3-1 in Copenhagen. Unfortunately, City lost to Chelsea in the two-legged final with Doyle missing both matches due to injury.

Mike Doyle was one of City's finest players under Mercer and Allison and later Tony Book, winning two League Cup Winners' medals, an FA Cup winners' medal and a European Cup-Winners' medal.

After Rodney Marsh left Maine Road in 1975, he was made club captain and a year later made the first of his five full international appearances for England against Wales. After struggling to get back into the City side after injury, he was transferred to Stoke City for £50,000 in June 1978 and played over 100 games for the Potters. He later played for both Bolton and Rochdale before retiring.

DRAWS

Manchester City played their greatest number of drawn league matches in a single season (18) in 1993-94 when they finished sixteenth in the Premier League and the fewest (2) in 1893-94, though that was from a 28-match programme. In 1959-60, the Blues only drew three of their 42 First Division matches.

The club's highest scoring draw is 4-4, a scoreline in two City matches: Everton (Home 1925-26) and Chelsea (Away 1936-37) although in a wartime game in December 1939, City drew 6-6 with Stockport County, Jimmy Heale scoring five of them.

The greatest number of drawn matches in a single Manchester City FA Cup tie is two. This happened in eight ties: Preston North End (1901-02); Sheffield United (1913-14); Halifax (1923-24); Cardiff City (1960-61) Everton (1965-66); Watford (1985-86) Huddersfield Town (1987-88) and Millwall (1989-90); It also occurred in four League Cup ties: Blackpool (1962-63); Walsall (1973-74); Norwich City (1975-76) and Luton Town (1977-78).

EARLY GROUNDS

Manchester City were originally called Ardwick F.C. a club formed in 1887 by the amalgamation of two teams: St Mark's (West Gorton) and Gorton Athletic. The former used a rough field at Clowes Street for their first season of 1880-81 a season later, they moved to Kirkmanshulme Cricket Club which was more centrally positioned in Gorton. But the cricketers objected to the damage to the turf, so they began their third season at Clemington Park called Dob Key Common. The renamed Gorton A. F.C, played at Pink Bank Lane which they rented for £6 per annum and in 1885-86 and again the following season, they rented a pitch at Reddish Lane from the landlord of the Bull's Head Hotel.

EUROPEAN CUP

City have participated in Europe's premier trophy on just one occasion and that was in 1968-69 following their success in winning the League title the previous season.

Drawn against Turkish champions Fenerbahce, the Blues played out a frustrating goal-less draw at Maine Road on 18th September 1968 this after Malcolm Allison had boasted City would terrorise Europe! The second leg was held at the National Stadium in Istanbul, when City gave up a one goal lead scored by Tony Coleman allowing Fenerbahce to win 2-1. The only consolation for City supporters was that the strong Turkish side had conceded only 12 goals in 34 matches.

EUROPEAN CUP-WINNERS' CUP

City made their debut in this competition in 1969-70, following their FA Cup success over Leicester City. Their opponents in the first round were Atletico Bilbao who were defeated 6-3 on aggregate. S.K. Lierse were beaten 8-0 over two legs with Francis Lee grabbing two goals in each match. In the third round, they had to rely on a Tony Towers' goal in the 209th and last minute of the two-legged match against Academica of Coimbra to progress into the semi-finals where they faced German side Schalke 04. Beaten 1-0 in the first leg, Joe Corrigan turned out with a broken nose to help City win 5-1 and reach the final.

The match took place on 29th April 1970 against Polish side Gornik Zabrze. A small crowd of 12,000 attended the final in Vienna, where it took City just twelve minutes for Neil Young to put his side ahead. Just before half-time, Young was upended in the penalty area and Lee blasted home the spot-kick. The Poles scored in the 68th minute but try as they might they couldn't snatch an equaliser and the European Cup-Winners' Cup was on its way to Maine Road.

The following season, City had to rely on away goals to put Irish club Linfield out in the first round, but then defeated Hungarian side Honved 3-0 on aggregate in the next round. In the third round they met Gornik Zabrze and after the first two matches had ended level on aggregate, they won the replay in Copenhagen 3-1 Unfortunately, the Blues lost to Chelsea in the semi-final, going down 1-0 in both legs.

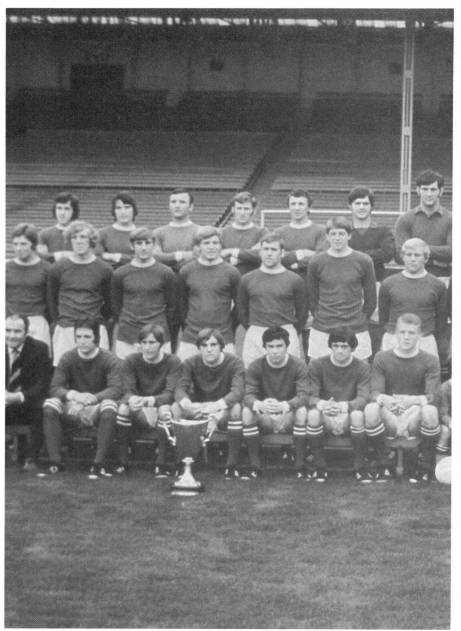

1970: with the Group League and European Cup Winners Cup Trophies

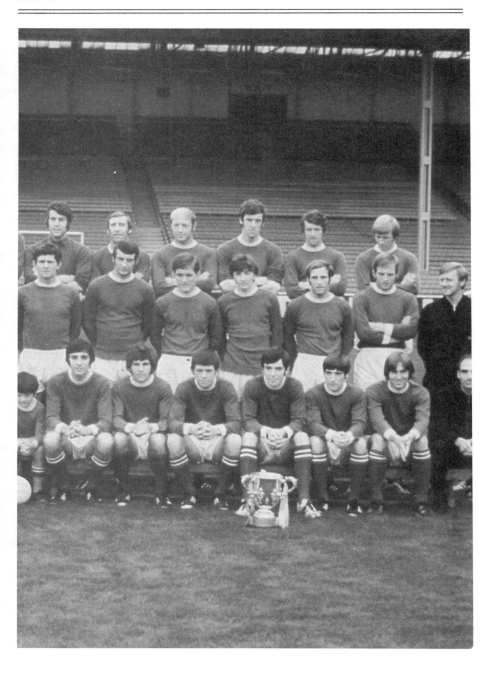

EVER PRESENTS

There have been fifty-six Manchester City players who have been ever present throughout a Football League season. The greatest number of ever-present seasons by a City player is five, the record being held by Eric Brook.

The full list is:

Number of Seasons:	Players:
5	E. Brook
4	J. Corrigan; W. Meredith; F. Swift;
3	S. Redmond; E. Toseland; B. Trautmann; C. Williams
2	S. Cookson; W. Donachie; J. Fagan; P. Finnerham
	R. Moffatt; P. Power; D. Robson; B. Smith; E. Westwood
	D. White; A. Williams
1	A. Barber; C. Bell; B. Betts; T. Book; K. Branagan
	T. Browell; J. Buchan; T. Caton; S. Cowan; G. Dorsett
	M. Doyle; D. Ewing; B. Gillespie; J. Goodchild
	J. Hayes; G. Hicks; T. Holford; W. Holmes; D. Jones
	B. Kennedy; F. Lee; B. Leivers; R. Little; N. McNab
	A. May; W. Murphy; J. Percival; D. Phillips; C. Pringle
	N. Quinn; R. Ray; K. Reeves; J. Ridley; W. Smith
	M. Summerbee; D. Wagstaffe; C. Wilson;

FATHER AND SON

Described by Denis Law as "the best uncapped wing-half who ever played in English football" Ken Barnes played for City from 1952 to 1961. His son Peter also wore the City colours – twice! – and went on to win international honours.

City's major signing during the 1993-94 close season was Nicky Summerbee for £1.5 million from Swindon Town. He followed in the footsteps of his famous father Mike when he joined the Blues. City manager John Bond (1980-83) signed his son Kevin from Seattle Sounders in September 1983.

FESTIVAL OF BRITAIN

On 9th May 1951, Manchester City entertained F.C. Wacker of Austria in the Festival of Britain game, City winning 2-1.

FILM STARS

City players Mike Summerbee and Kaziu Deyna hit the cinema screens in a wartime escape epic entitled "Escape to Victory" which also featured Bobby Moore and Brazilian star, Pele.

FINES

The most severe penalty ever imposed on a club was against Manchester City in 1906. City players, including Billy Meredith were accused of offering inducements to an Aston Villa player to throw a game on 29th April 1905. Villa eventually won that game 32. At the time City were running neck-and-neck with Newcastle United for the Championship. The City team had been offered a £100 bonus (a massive sum at the time) to win the game and the club had been consistently in the breach of the 1901 rules on maximum bonuses that could be offered to players. City were fined £250 but that was irrelevant compared with the other penalties.

The secretary and chairman were suspended until 1st January 1907, forbidden to ever play for City again and were auctioned off. Billy Meredith was probably lucky to get away with such lenient treatment, particularly as he was later reported for trying to obtain wages and bonuses from City while under suspension.

FIRE

A fire on the night of 6th November 1920 destroyed City's Hyde Road Ground Main Stand. The cause was not, as might be thought, a stray firework, but a cigarette end.

All the club's records perished in the fire, as did their faithful watch-dog "Nell" an Airedale terrier.

FIRST DIVISION

Promoted to the First Division at the end of the 1898-99 season, the Blues only lasted three seasons before being relegated. However, within a season they were back in the top flight.

In 1903-04 City won their first four games and ended the season as runners-up in Division One. The following season the Blues finished a respectable third and were fifth in 1905-06. Relegated to the Second Division in 1908-09 they soon shot back to the First Division and spent the next 12 seasons in Division One, five before World War One and seven afterwards. During this period they were reliant on goals from Tommy Browell and Horace Barnes. The club's best performance in this spell was to finish runners-up in 1920-21 when the club did not suffer a single home defeat. Relegated in 1925-26, the Blues only needed two seasons in Division Two before they returned to the First Division. They scored a creditable 95 goals of which Tommy Johnson hit 38. Examples of his scoring ability included five goals in the 6-2 thrashing of Everton.

In 1936-37, City won their first-ever League Championship finishing three points ahead of Charlton Athletic. They lost only one home match, 4-2 against Sunderland in October 1936. Yet surprisingly, they were relegated the following season – the only instance of this happening in the Football League.

The Blues next season in the top flight was 1947-48, but after three campaigns they were relegated. However, as on two other occasions, they bounced straight back into the First Division. In 1955-56 City finished fourth in Division One, but the usual eccentricities were waiting to re-appear. They were grateful to avoid relegation the next season before climbing back to fifth in 1957-58. It was a season in which they scored 104 goals and conceded 100. It is the only occasion a team has scored and conceded a century of goals in a Football League season. Relegated in 1962-63, City spent three seasons in the Second Division, but it was a prelude to an era of the club's greatest achievements. In 1967-68, City won their second League Championship after winning 4-3 at Newcastle in the final game of the season. City played in the First Division for seventeen consecutive seasons, their longest stay in the top flight. Following relegation in 1982-83, the Blues spent only two seasons in Division Two before returning to the First Division. Two years later they were back in the Second

Division but another period of two years saw them return to Division One. City's last season in the First Division was 1991-92 when they finished fifth.

City's full league record in the First Division is:

P.	W.	D.	L.	F.	A.
2772	1061	677	1034	4277	4232

FLOODLIGHTS

Floodlights were installed in 1953 and officially switched on 14th October that year for a friendly match against Hearts, City winning 6-3. This innovation brought Manchester United back to Maine Road for a series of mid-week matches in various competitions, until Old Trafford had its own lights in 1957. In 1956, Maine Road became the first English ground to stage European Cup football, when United beat RSC Anderlecht 10-0 under City's floodlights.

In 1963-64, the floodlighting system was sold to non-league Leamington and replaced with four very tall pylons visible from miles around, plus another smaller gantry on the Kippax Street roof.

FOOTBALL ASSOCIATION CUP

Manchester City have won the FA Cup on four occasions. They first entered the competition in 1890-91 and their match in the qualifying round saw them beat Liverpool Stanley 12-0. It is the club's best win in the FA Cup, but despite the margin of victory, they scratched from the following round.

Before their first appearance in the FA Cup Final in 1904, City had experienced very little success at national level. Turnbull, Gillespie and Meredith played a major role in the club reaching the Final and it was Meredith's goal that defeated Bolton Wanderers to give City their first FA Cup success.

In the 1912-13 competition, City defeated Birmingham 4-0 in round one and drew Sunderland at home in the next. The Hyde Road ground was the venue. The spectators were crammed onto the terraces and people began spilling on to the pitch. As a result the game which was goal-less to that point was abandoned in extra time. The FA fined Manchester City £500 and to make matters worse, they lost 2-0 in the replay at Sunderland.

The 1923-24 season was an important one in terms of the FA Cup. City beat Nottingham Forest 2-1 and then fought it out with Halifax Town until they won 3-0 after two replays. Beating Brighton 5-1 and Cardiff 1-0 after a replay, they met Newcastle United in the semi-final. Recalled to the side at almost fifty years of age, Billy Meredith was hoping to provide scoring opportunities for the forwards, but it wasn't to be and City lost 2-0.

City reached Wembley for the first time in 1926 (their previous Final appearance having been at Crystal Palace) where again their opponents were Bolton Wanderers. Facing the renowned amateur side Corinthians, the Blues drew 3-3 but won the replay 4-0. Huddersfield Town were beaten by the same score and in round five, Crystal Palace visited Maine Road. In this incredible game, City were leading 7-0 at half-time and finished winning 11-4. After beating Second Division Clapton Orient in the sixth round, City played United in an all Manchester semi-final at Bramall Lane. Two goals from Tommy Browell and one from Frank Roberts took the Blues to Wembley. It wasn't to be the same outcome as the 1904 Final, David Jack scoring the only goal of the game to give Bolton victory.

The early 1930s provided the Maine Road faithful with plenty of success in the FA Cup. In 1931-32 City reached the FA Cup semi-final only to lose 1-0 to Arsenal in a most remarkable way. In the last minute, Arsenal's Cliff Bastin's shot was parried away by Langford in the City goal, only for the ball to then hit the crossbar, shoot back to the line, bounce off an upright and enter the net!

The following season City reached Wembley for a second time, beating Gateshead 9-0 on the way after the two sides had drawn 1-1. Their opponents in the Final were Everton. Led by Dixie Dean, the Toffees were the best team on the day and won 3-0. City returned to the Twin Towers in 1934 to face Portsmouth. In the sixth round they beat Stoke City 1-0 in front of a crowd of 84,569 at Maine Road. In the Final, two goals from Fred Tilson gave City victory 2-1.

In 1955 City reached Wembley again beating Manchester United 2-0 on their way. Unfortunately for the Blues they lost Jimmy Meadows and reduced to ten men went down 3-1 to Newcastle United. But,

Manchester City v Birmingham, FA Cup Final, 1956

as in the thirties, the Blues were back at Wembley the following year. On their way the team endured some dreadful weather conditions with the Blackpool game having to be abandoned because of a blanket of fog. Replayed the following week, City won 2-1 on a mud-bath of a pitch at Maine Road. Following a goal-less draw at home to Liverpool, the Blues travelled to a snow-covered Anfield and won 2-1. Facing Birmingham in the Final, City won 3-1 with goals from Hayes, Dyson and Johnstone.

The following season saw a really exciting FA Cup match between City and Newcastle United. Having drawn 1-1 at St James' Park, the Blues were confident in the replay, especially after going 3-0 up after twenty-five minutes. But in a second half completely dominated by the Magpies, the full-time score was 3-3. Johnstone made it 4-3 to City early in extra-time, but two late goals by Len White gave Newcastle a 5-4 win!

In 1969 City won through to the Final again but only after teenager

Tommy Booth had scored the crucial goal in the closing moments of the semi-final with Everton. Facing Leicester City in the Final, it took a fine strike from Neil Young to take the Cup back to Maine Road for the first time in 13 years.

City's last visit to Wembley for an FA Cup Final was in 1981 when Malcolm Allison's Crystal Palace were beaten in the third round 4-0 and John Bond's former Norwich side in the fourth 6-0. Beating Peterborough and Everton albeit after a replay, the Blues faced Ipswich in the semi-final. An extra-time goal by Paul Power put City into the Final against Spurs. Tommy Hutchinson scored for both sides and the 1-1 result necessitated a replay. A thrilling match followed with Spurs winning 3-2, Ricky Villa scoring an exciting individual goal in the closing minutes.

FOOTBALL ASSOCIATION CUP FINALS

Manchester City's first final appearance was in 1904 when 61,374 attended the Crystal Palace venue where the Blues defeated Bolton Wanderers 1-0 with a controversial Billy Meredith goal. Receiving a Livingstone pass, Meredith weaved among several Bolton defenders before hitting the ball home from 12 yards. Bolton fans thought he was offside, but the referee did not blow and so Meredith it was who received the FA Cup from Lord Alfred Lyttleton.

Bolton Wanderers were City's opponents in 1926 when the Blues next reached the Final. Even though Bolton controlled the opening twenty minutes or so, half-time arrived goal-less. However, with just thirteen minutes remaining, David Jack hit home a left-foot shot for the only goal of the game to take the Cup to Bolton.

The 1933 Cup Final was the first of two consecutive Wembley appearances for the Maine Road club, who were meeting Everton for the first time in an FA Cup tie. It was the first time that City had turned out in numbered shirts and in order to avoid a colour clash with Everton, they wore a red and white strip. Although there was no score until the 40th minute, City went down 3-0. City returned to Wembley in 1934 where two late goals from Fred Tilson, who had missed the final the year before, swung the game their way.

Returning to Wembley in 1955, City were a goal down to Newcastle

United within the first minute and a short time later, Jimmy Meadows was forced to retire. Even though reduced to ten men, City equalised when Bobby Johnstone headed home Hayes' cross. However two Newcastle goals in the second half took the Cup to the North East – the third FA Cup victory for Newcastle in a five-year period. Twelve months later, City returned to Wembley to face Birmingham City. Keeping the ball on the floor, they built up the attacks in an almost lazy manner. Within three minutes, Joe Hayes' splendid left foot volley made it 1-0 for City. Kinsey equalised for Birmingham but the Blues hit back to score a couple of incredible goals in the space of two minutes! Of course, the 1956 Wembley game with Birmingham will be remembered for Bert Trautmann's bravery. He valiantly played the last fifteen minutes with a broken neck.

Back at Wembley after an absence of 13 years, City were expected to annihilate a Leicester side almost certain of relegation. As it was, the only goal of the game came when long-striding Neil Young drilled a well-aimed volley into the roof of the net. The Centenary FA Cup Final of 1981 saw City and Spurs produce one of the most entertaining of Wembley matches ever. Tommy Hutchinson gave the Blues a 1-0 lead but with just ten minutes left, Hutchinson deflected Hoddle's free-kick for Tottenham's equaliser. Until that moment, Joe Corrigan had looked unbeatable. In the replay, Corrigan was beaten three times, twice by Ricky Villa, whose deciding goal was one of the best ever seen in a Cup Final and though MacKenzie and Reeves scored for City, it was not enough.

FOOTBALLER OF THE YEAR

The Football Writers' Footballer of the Year award has been won by Manchester City players on three occasions.

Past winners have been:

1955	Don Revie
1956	Bert Trautmann
1969	Tony Book (shared with Dave Mackay)

FOOTBALL LEAGUE CUP

Sad to relate, City have failed to make much impact upon the Football League (later Milk, Littlewoods, Rumblelows and Coca Cola) Cup in recent years. However, in the seventies, it was a different story.

City's first game in the competition took place on 18th October 1960 at Maine Road when neighbours Stockport County were beaten 3-0. City's best performance in the early years of the competition was reaching the semi-final in 1963-64 where they went out 2-1 on aggregate to Stoke City.

The Blues first won the trophy in 1969-70. They started by beating Southport 3-0 and then Liverpool 3-2. In the next round they faced Everton and won 2-0 with goals from Bell and Lee. The next team to be beaten by City were Queen's Park Rangers who lost 3-0 at Maine Road. The two-legged semi-final against neighbours Manchester

After the 1970 Cup Final. Left to right: Joe Corrigan, Francis Lee,
Tony Book (with cup), George Heslop and Glyn Pardoe

United saw City win the first leg at Maine Road 2-1 thanks to a late Francis Lee penalty. In the second leg United led 2-1 with just minutes remaining when City were awarded an indirect free-kick on the edge of the box. Francis Lee thundered a shot at goal, Stepney rather surprisingly parried it and Summerbee knocked home the rebound.

Facing West Bromwich Albion in the Final, the Blues had to go into extra-time. It was Glyn Pardoe who emerged as the unlikely match winner as his shot beat Osborne in the West Brom nets after twelve minutes of extra-time. City reached the League Cup Final for a second time in 1973-74 only to lose 2-1 to Wolverhampton Wanderers. The club's third appearance in the Final in seven years came in 1975-76. The Blues had beaten Norwich City, Nottingham Forest, Manchester United, Mansfield Town and Middlesbrough before meeting Newcastle United at Wembley. Peter Barnes opened the scoring before Gowling equalised for the Magpies. There then came a spectacular overhead kick by City's Dennis Tueart that settled the issue and brought the Cup back to Maine Road.

City reached the semi-final stage in 1980-81 only to lose 2-1 on aggregate to Liverpool. In the first leg at Maine Road which City lost 1-0, Kevin Reeves appeared to have a perfectly good goal disallowed.

The club's best run in recent years was last season when the Blues reached the fifth round, only to lose 4-0 to Crystal Palace at Selhurst Park.

City's record to date in the League Cup is:

P.	W.	D.	L.	F.	A.
147	78	31	38	258	165

FOREIGN PLAYERS

Probably the club's first foreign player was Walter Bowman, a member of the Canadian touring team that played Ardwick on 12th December 1891. He decided to stay in this country after his teammates had returned home. Another foreign player arrived prior to the First World War and that was Dutch international Nico Bouvy, but he played in just two Reserve games before returning home on the outbreak of war.

Bremen-born Bert Trautmann was a former German paratrooper and ex-Prisoner of War, but soon won over the hearts of the City fans as he went on to make 545 first-team appearances between 1949 and 1964. The next to arrive was New York-born striker Gerry Baker who signed from St Mirren in 1960, but despite scoring 14 times in 39 senior games he moved on to Hibernian after a year. South African

Kaziu Deyna

born Colin Viljoen cost City £100,000 from Ipswich Town but he too left the club after a short time to join Chelsea. Poland's Kaziu Deyna had won 102 international caps when he signed for City in November 1978. He scored some wonderful goals for the club, but on John Bond's arrival, he moved to California, sadly to die in a car crash in September 1989. Another of Malcolm Allison's signings was the Yugoslavian defender Dragoslav Stepanovic. It was pointed out to the City boss that the Yugoslav's English was limited to say the least. The cigar-smoking City boss is reputed to have indicated that the team would just have to learn the Serbo-Croat!

The first Norwegian player to play for City was Aage Hareide who joined the club in October 1981, followed just over eleven years later by Kare Ingebrigtsen. He found himself in and out of favour and returned to Norway on loan. When he returned he scored a hat-trick in an FA Cup tie against Leicester City.

Perhaps the biggest disappointment of all City's foreign players was Ivan Golac. The former Southampton full-back stayed for a month and played in two League games, both of which City lost 4-1. Dutchman Danny Hoekman gave some great displays in the reserve side but after just three appearances as substitute he was released. City's third Dutchman Michel Vonk made his full debut against Chelsea in

1992 and is still with the club. Another Dutchman Alfons Groenendijk joined the club in July 1993 but after 12 appearances moved to Sparta Rotterdam.

German Steffen Karl wasn't at City for long but did score an invaluable goal at The Dell in April 1994 to help keep City in the Premiership. Uwe Rosler is probably the most exciting of all the foreign players to have graced Maine Road, along with Maurizio Gaudino, while City's latest foreign signings are Georgiou Kinkladze from Dynamo Tblisi and goalkeeper Eike Immel from Stuttgart.

City have had on their books some players who, though not born on foreign shores, had very foreign-sounding names – notably Dave Bacuzzi, Peter Bodak and, of course, Imre Varadi!

FRIENDLIES

Since the opening of Maine Road in August 1923, Manchester City have played host to a number of opponents in friendly matches. Below is a full list of all City's home matches in this category when foreign opposition visited Maine Road.

Date	Opponents	Result	Score
24.11.1924	South African XI	Won	3-1
18.12.1933	F. K. Austria Vienna	Won	3-0
13.11.1935	Slovan Sparta	Won	4-1
09.05.1951	F.C. Wacker	Won	2-1
02.02.1952	River Plate F.C.	Lost	3-4
21.10.1953	Fenerbahce	Won	5-1
25.11.1953	F.C. Wacker	Won	3-2
06.12.1956	MTK-VM	Lost	2-3
11.03.1957	SV Werder Bremen	Won	4-0
11.10.1961	Torino	Won	4-3
06.12.1965	Dinamo Moscow	Won	2-0
11.08.1967	Borussia Dortmund	Won	4-0
31.10.1968	Ajax, Amsterdam	Won	3-0
25.11.1970	Australian Tourists	Won	2-0
21.09.1971	Hertha BSC	Drew	1-1
08.11.1979	Werder Bremen	Won	4-0
12.08.1980	Legia, Warsaw	Lost	1-5
14.11.1984	Australian XI	Lost	1-3
05.08.1987	PSV Eindhoven	Won	3-1

FRIZZELL, JIMMY

Jimmy Frizzell made his name by taking Oldham Athletic from the Fourth to the Second Division. He spent 22 years at Boundary Park as player, coach and manager. Originally an inside-forward, he scored 24 goals in 1961-62; he later played at wing-half and full-back. In 1968 he became the club coach and took over as caretaker manager in December 1969 before being permanently appointed three months later.

Oldham soon won promotion from Division Four and were Third Division champions in 1973-74, but with the club still in the Second Division he was surprisingly sacked in June 1982.

He had been out of work for a year when he accepted Billy McNeill's offer to be his assistant at Maine Road. When McNeill moved to Villa Park, Frizzell took over, but was working on a tight financial budget. He could do little to halt the slide and when City were finally relegated, he was moved to the post of general manager.

City's full League record under Jimmy Frizzell is:

P.	W.	D.	L.	F.	A.
39	7	14	18	33	55

FULL MEMBERS' CUP

Entering the above competition for the first time in 1985-86, City reached the Final. In their group matches they beat Leeds United 6-1 with Gordon Davies scoring a hat-trick and Sheffield United 2-1. A goal-less draw with Sunderland was settled by penalties and then the Blues took on Hull City in the Northern Final. In the first match at Boothferry Park they lost 2-1 but in the second leg at Maine Road they won 2-0 to give them a 3-2 win on aggregate.

A superb final against Chelsea at Wembley resulted in a 5-4 victory for the London side, despite City taking an early lead.

The following season, City beat Wimbledon 3-1 and Watford 1-0 to progress to round four, where in spite of two Imre Varadi goals they went out of the competition 3-2 at home to Ipswich Town.

FURNISS, LAWRENCE

An amateur forward with Gorton FC, he joined the City club when the two Gorton sides merged in 1883. A serious knee injury ended his playing career and so he moved into the administrative side of the game.

He was the man who brought Billy Meredith to the club after spotting him play for Northwich when refereeing a match involving the club. Furniss also travelled to Scotland to sign a number of players from north of the border during his spell as manager at Hyde Road. He also brought several Bolton players to the club, notably David Weir, Wanderers' international forward.

He was a great servant to the club, playing a big part in City's early growth to become one of the country's leading sides. Eventually giving way to Joshua Parlby, he remained with City for 46 years in the capacity of director, chairman and eventually club president.

City's full League record under Lawrence Furniss is:

P.	W.	D.	L.	F.	A.
22	9	3	10	45	40

GAINSBOROUGH TRINITY

They spent sixteen seasons, all in the Second Division between 1896 and 1912 without ever managing to finish any higher than sixth.

The two clubs met on ten occasions with City winning all their home matches, including a 9-0 victory on 28th February 1903 with Jimmy Bannister scoring three. They last met in 1909-10 with City winning both games 3-1 with Billy Lot Jones scoring all three in the away fixture.

GILLESPIE, BILLY

A bustling, determined centre-forward, Billy Gillespie thrived on the service provided by Meredith, Threlfall and later Booth. Over a period of eight years with the club, Gillespie scored 132 goals in 213 League and FA Cup appearances.

Joining City from Lincoln in January 1897, the Strathclyde-born Gillespie scored on his debut in a 3-1 defeat at Darwen. Though he soon earned himself the reputation of being a "bad boy" on the pitch, his skill and good humour endeared him to the City fans. Gillespie scored a hat-trick in the 7-2 win over Grimsby Town on the opening day of the 1898-99 season and in the penultimate game of the 1901-02 campaign scored all four goals as City won at Blackburn Rovers 4-1. In his time with City, Gillespie helped the club to two Second Division championships and victory in the 1904 FA Cup Final.

In the summer of 1905 he decided to leave English football and emigrated according to one newspaper report "to the diamond fields of South Africa". Even then Gillespie's reputation was maintained, when, a year after he had sailed for Cape Town, the FA decided to fine him £50 and suspend him following alleged transfer irregularities!

GLOSSOP NORTH END

Finishing runners-up to City at the end of their first season in the League, 1898-99, they were promoted to the First Division. The two clubs first met in that season on 12th November 1898 when goals from Meredith and Gillespie gave City a 2-1 win at Glossop. In the First Division City completed the double over Glossop as the Derby-shire side were immediately relegated. The two clubs next met in 1902-03 when City won 1-0 away and 5-2 at home with Billy Gillespie hitting a hat-trick. Glossop finished bottom of the table in the last season before World War One, 1914-15 and resigned from the League shortly before the resumption of matches in 1919.

GOAL AVERAGE

Goal average which was replaced by goal difference in 1976-77 was established by dividing the number of goals a team scored by those conceded. The first time it was required to decide the champions of a Football League division was in 1895-96 when Liverpool took the Second Division title from Manchester City with an average of 3.31 to City's 1.66.

GOALKEEPERS

Manchester City have almost always been extremely well served by their goalkeepers and most of them have been highly popular with the supporters.

Frank Swift was one of the best goalkeepers of his generation and was the club's first choice 'keeper from the 1933-34 season until his retirement in 1949. Following his debut on Christmas Day 1933 he went on to make 195 consecutive appearances. He also holds the record for the longest unbeaten spell between one goal and the next conceded by a goalkeeper, which covered a period of five clean sheets from 28th December 1946 to 22nd February 1947.

Bert Trautmann is the legendary City figure, disgracefully never capped by his country. He holds the club record for the most league appearances, 508, between 1949 and 1964 and broke his neck in City's cause in the 1956 FA Cup Final.

Joe Corrigan holds the club record for the most first-team appearances in League and Cup competitions with 592 between 1969 and 1983 and also the number of clean sheets in a season with 22 in 1976-77.

City goalkeeper Jack Hillman was one of the great footballers of his day. There is a story that on one occasion he accepted a wager to keep goal one-handed in a charity match – and helped his team win 1-0.

City's amateur goalkeeper Jim Mitchell always played in spectacles.

On 14th April 1900, City went down 3-1 to Sunderland in a game where the Blues 'keeper Charlie Williams blasted the ball down the pitch. Aided by a strong gust of wind, it beat Scottish international goalkeeper Doig and gave City a consolation goal! Harry Dowd once broke a finger in a match against Bury. He moved to centre-forward and gained a point when he scored City's equaliser in the 83rd minute.

GOAL-SCORING

For the club:

City's highest goal-scoring tallies were achieved in 1926-27 when the team that finished third in the Second Division hit 108 League goals in 42 matches and in 1936-37 when the Blues scored 107 goals to win the First Division championship.

By the individual:

The following players have scored 50 or more League goals for the club:

Eric Brook	(1928-1940)	159
Tom Johnson	(1919-1930)	158
Billy Meredith	(1894-1906) and (1921-1924)	145
Joe Hayes	(1953-1965)	142
Billy Gillespie	(1897-1905)	126
Tom Browell	(1913-1926)	122
Horace Barnes	(1914-1924)	120
Colin Bell	(1966-1979)	117
Frank Roberts	(1922-1929)	116
Francis Lee	(1967-1974)	112
Fred Tilson	(1928-1938)	110
Alex Herd	(1933-1948)	107
Irvine Thornley	(1904-1912)	92
Dennis Tueart	(1974-1978) and (1980-1983)	86
Neil Young	(1959-1972)	86
Colin Barlow	(1956-1963)	78
David White	(1986-1994)	78
Peter Doherty	(1936-1945)	76
George Smith	(1938-1951)	75
Roy Clarke	(1947-1958)	73
Bob Marshall	(1928-1939)	70
Billy Jones	(1903-1919)	69
Johnny Hart	(1944-1963)	67
George Dorsett	(1904-1912)	62
Billy McAdams	(1953-1960)	62
Ernie Toseland	(1929-1939)	61
Niall Quinn	(1989-1995)	58
George Wynn	(1909-1919)	54
Sandy Turnbull	(1902-1906)	53

All dates refer to calendar year debuts and last appearances. Correct to August 1995.

GORTON AFC

In 1883-84 West Gorton and Gorton Athletic joined forces and it soon became clear that a new name was needed for the club. So in 1884-85 the Gorton Association Football Club was formed. Playing its matches on a pitch in Pink Bank Lane, Gorton, they only lost two of their 16 fixtures that season.

The club moved from Pink Bank Lane to play their games on a pitch on Reddish Lane in 1885-86 but had to pay the landlord of the Bull's Head Pub for the use of the land.

GUEST PLAYERS

The "guest" system was used by all clubs during the two wars. Although at times it was abused almost beyond belief (in that some sides that opposed City had ten or eleven "guests"!) it normally worked sensibly and effectively, to the benefit of players, clubs and supporters alike.

The most distinguished player to "guest" for Manchester City was Johnny Carey, who along with his United colleagues Stan Pearson and Harry McShane all managed to get their names on the City score sheet.

In the Second World War, Andy Black "guested" for Chester and Portsmouth. He appeared for Pompey in the London War Cup Final and in one match against Clapham Orient scored 8 goals! Eric Westwood "guested" for Chelsea and appeared in the 1944 War Cup Final.

HART, JOHNNY

Johnny Hart was a great servant to Manchester City but, largely due to a succession of injuries, in 16 years at Maine Road he made only 178 appearances, scoring 73 goals. A broken leg at Huddersfield just before City's appearance in the 1955 FA Cup Final was a cruel blow for him. He never re-established himself after this, making only 11 more appearances before retiring.

asf

He then spent a decade on the Maine Road staff before becoming manager after the departure of Malcolm Allison. Hart signed Denis Law on a free transfer from Manchester United during his period as manager, but after only six months in charge, he was forced to give the position up due to ill health. Hart later returned to Maine Road in the late 1980s to work on the promotional side of the club.

City's full League record under Johnny Hart is:

Johnny Hart

P.	W.	D.	L.	F.	A.
27	12	7	8	30	37

Asa Hartford

HARTFORD, ASA

Born in Clydebank, Asa Hartford was named after the celebrated America singer Al Jolson.

He was plucked from Scottish amateur football after being spotted by a West Bromwich Albion scout and signed professional forms for them in 1967, playing for them in the League Cup Final some three years later. He was soon thrilling the crowds with his mature skill and vision and it was only a matter of time before the inevitable big-money offer arrived to tempt Albion.

a Hartford and team-mates line up for a 1977 shot. Picture by the Manchester Evening News.

Hartford will probably always be remembered as the player whose transfer to then First Division giants, Leeds United, was sensationally called off after a routine medical examination revealed a hole-in-the-heart condition. That was in 1972, when he was poised to move from the Hawthorns to Elland Road for £170,000. Showing great durability, the condition, happily for Asa was a minor one and in August 1974, he joined Manchester City for £225,000. Making his debut against West Ham United, he swept away all doubts about his fitness with his stamina and urgent play in midfield. He went on to play a major role in City's glorious era of the late-1970s, picking up a League Cup winners' medal with them in 1976.

In June 1979 he signed for Nottingham Forest, under the management of Brian Clough for £500,000 but after only 63 days and three league games, he was on his way back to the north-west and Everton.

Hartford was a wily character, quick of temper and determined, but also gifted and the kind of midfield terrier every successful team needs. After two seasons and 98 appearances for Everton, he moved back to Manchester City for £350,000 and a second spell. When City bought him for the second time, he was still a current Scottish international player. He won 50 Scottish caps, 36 of them in his time with City.

After 318 first-team games and 36 goals, the tough, selfless player crossed the Atlantic to join the ranks of the soccer team, Fort Lauderdale Sun. He later returned to First Division action with Norwich City, helping them win the Milk Cup in 1985, when his shot was deflected by Sunderland's Chisholm for the only goal of the game. Granted a free-transfer he joined Bolton Wanderers, where he became club captain and a great inspiration. Player-manager of Stockport County and manager of Shrewsbury, he then worked for Blackburn and Stoke before returning to Maine Road for a third time as Alan Ball's second-in-command.

HAT-TRICKS

Manchester City have netted 134 hat-tricks in Football League games with Billy Meredith, Tommy Browell and Fred Tilson sharing the record with six each, closely followed by Irvine Thornley with five.

The club's first hat-trick in the Football League came on the opening day of the 1892-93 season when J. Davies hit three goals in the 7-0 win over Bootle. Other debutants to score on their league debut include F. Howard who scored all four goals in the 4-1 victory over Liverpool on 18th January 1913 and Jimmy Constantine on 14th September 1946 as City beat Millwall 3-0 at the Den. Although 29 players have joined the exclusive hat-trick club since the war for City, it is surprising to find the likes of Joe Hayes who scored 142 League goals for City, managed only one hat-trick, that coming against Bolton Wanderers in a 4-2 win on 16th March 1955.

There have been three occasions when two City players have scored hat-tricks in the same league match. The first came on 3rd September 1898 when Meredith (3) and Gillespie (3) helped City to a 7-2 win over Grimsby Town. Later that season, F. Williams (5) and Meredith (3) scored in City's 10-0 home win over Darwen. In 1963-64 Gray (3) and Kevan (3) scored hat-tricks as City beat Scunthorpe United 8-1. The fifth and last instance in the history of the Football League of three players from one side scoring hat-tricks in the same game came on 7th November 1987 when City beat Huddersfield Town 10-1 at Maine Road. City's hat-trick heroes were Adcock, Stewart and White.

Tom Holford hit three hat-tricks within the space of twenty-one days in January 1909, whilst Imre Varadi hit a double hat-trick in a pre-season game against Lovangers in July 1987. Colin Barlow is the only other City player to hit six goals in a tour game abroad.

Perhaps the most unusual hat-trick was scored by Ken Barnes, who converted three penalties in City's 6-2 win over Everton in December 1957.

HAYES, JOE

Arriving at Maine Road with his boots in a brown-paper parcel, Joe Hayes proceeded to score four goals in a trial game for Manchester

City. Within eight weeks he was making his league debut in City's 3-0 defeat against Tottenham Hotspur at White Hart Lane.

Working at a local colliery and then in a cotton mill before signing for the Blues in August 1953, Hayes overcame poor eyesight to become one of the club's best goal-poachers in the post-war era. In 363 first-team games for the club, he scored 152 goals. Playing for Young England, England Under-23s and the FA XI, Hayes also

Joe Hayes

appeared for City in two FA Cup Finals, with a winners' medal in 1956 when he scored in the Blues 3-1 win over Birmingham City.

There is no doubt his goal tally for City would have been much higher but for a serious knee injury sustained at Gigg Lane on 28th September 1963. In June 1965, Hayes left Maine Road to join Barnsley on a free-transfer before ending his career at Wigan Athletic and Lancaster City, where he was player-manager.

HEALEY CHARITY CUP

Manchester City won this trophy three times at the turn of the century, beating Newton Heath 4-2 in 1897-98 and 2-1 win 1898-99 and Stockport County 5-1 in 1900-01.

HERD, ALEX

Signed from Scottish club Hamilton Academicals, Alex Herd had a dramatic entry into English football, for within 15 months, he had played in two FA Cup Finals for Manchester City.

A member of one of the club's greatest-ever teams, he starred in the 1936-37 side which won the League Championship, making 32 appearances and scoring 15 goals. A deep-lying inside-forward he would carry the ball forward before releasing it to send his fellow-strikers Tilson, Doherty and Brook to shoot for goal.

Alex Herd's career stretched into wartime football and in 1942 he was capped by Scotland. When peacetime football resumed, Herd was still at Maine Road and won a Second Division championship medal in 1946-47.

His son, David went on to win honours with Manchester United. Alex Herd left City for Stockport County on a free-transfer in March 1948 and on the last day of the 1950-51 season he turned out alongside his son when they were County's inside-forwards against Hartlepool United.

HMS MANCHESTER

In August 1985, the City Youth team beat a team from the *HMS Manchester* by 13-0. Paul Molden came on as substitute and scored 5 goals in twenty minutes.

HODGE, PETER

Entering football administration in his home town of Dunfermline with a local boys' club, he was later involved with Dunfermline Juniors and Athletic before becoming manager of Raith Rovers, who he took into the First Division.

In June 1914, Hodge came to England and took over at Stoke, then a Southern League Second Division club, before guiding them into the Football League. During the war he returned to Scotland to manage Raith Rovers again and was the local recruitment officer for the armed forces. He returned to English football in 1919 as Leicester manager and saw them into the First Division, before accepting Manchester City's offer in 1926.

His move came as something of a shock because City had just been relegated to Division Two. In his first season in charge, City just missed out on promotion by one place in the narrowest promotion race margin ever, goal-average to the third decimal place, but were promoted as champions in 1927-28 and finished third in the First Division the following season.

During his reign at Maine Road, several notable players became established in the side including Eric Brook and Tommy Johnson. Attracted by a five-year contract, he returned to manage Leicester in 1932.

City's full League record under Peter Hodge is:

P.	W.	D.	L.	F.	A.
252	115	59	78	562	430

HOME MATCHES

Not including the pre-football League matches, City's best home wins have been the 11-3 victory over Lincoln City in a Division Two match on 23rd March 1895, the 12-0 victory over Liverpool Stanley in a qualifying round of the FA Cup in October 1890 and the 11-4 win over Crystal Palace in an FA Cup fourth round tie on 20th February 1926. In 1898-99, City beat Darwen 10-0 in a Division Two fixture and Swindon Town 10-1 in the FA Cup whilst more recently they beat Huddersfield Town 10-1 on 7th November 1987.

City have scored nine goals at home on three occasions: Burton Swifts 9-0 in 1897-98; Gainsborough Trinity 9-0 in 1902-03 and Gateshead 9-0 in 1932-33.

City's worst home defeat was 7-2 against West Bromwich Albion on New Year's Day 1934. They have also conceded six goals at home on four occasions: Aston Villa 2-6 in 1911-12; Millwall 1-6 in 1938-39; Blackpool 1-6 in 1954-55 and Wolves 4-6 in 1959-60.

The highest scoring home match other than those mentioned above is City's 8-3 victory over Burnley on 24th October 1925 – they then proceeded to lose their next match away to Sheffield United by the same score!

HOME SEASONS

Manchester City have gone through a complete League season with an undefeated home record on four occasions. In 1895-96, City won 12 and drew 3 of their 15 matches: in 1904-05 they won 14 and drew 3 and in 1920-21 they won 19 and drew 2 of their 21 matches. In 1965-66 they won 14 and drew 7 of their home matches in winning the Second Division championship.

The club's highest number of home wins in a League season is 18. They achieved this number of victories in 1927-28 when winning the Second Division title. They also scored 100 league goals, 70 of them coming at Maine Road – another record.

HORTON, BRIAN

As a player, Brian Horton was a master of the well-timed tackle and interception. At Brighton he was synonymous with the club's rise from the Third to the First Division in the late 1970s. He also captained Luton Town to the Second Division championship in 1981-82.

Managerial responsibilities affected his displays on the field at Hull City, but he took them to promotion to Division Two in 198485. A poor run of results cost him his job in 1988 and he moved to Oxford United to become assistant to Mark Lawrenson. When the former Liverpool star resigned, Horton took over. The club struggled for survival, especially after the death of Robert Maxwell and they had to sell most of their best players to survive as the club were left with huge debts.

On 27th August 1993, Brian Horton was the surprise new appointment at Manchester City as police quelled an angry demonstration against chairman Peter Swales. He eventually departed following a takeover by former Maine Road idol Francis Lee. There were many personnel changes in Brian Horton's first season in charge, but the Blues experienced a flying start with six points and six goals in the two opening games. However, the rest of the season was a fight as City struggled to retain their premiership status. The following season wasn't much different and this signalled the end of Horton's 21-month reign as City's manager.

City's full League record under Brian Horton is:

P.	W.	D.	L.	F.	A.
84	21	32	31	91	113

HYDE ROAD

This was the club's first properly enclosed ground. It was a large ground, but hemmed in by the railway to the west and sidings to the north and railway drivers would often slow down as they went past for a quick view of the game. Hyde Road was visited by King Edward VII and Prime Minister A.J. Balfour, an occasion very nearly ruined when a small fire broke out in the Main Stand.

During the First World War, Hyde Road was used for stabling 300 horses and City carried on using it for their Lancashire Combination games. However, it was becoming apparent that the ground was no longer adequate for the growing number of supporters and it was planned for City to move to nearby Belle Vue, a large pleasure park. But the site available was only eight acres and City wanted somewhere larger.

The club soldiered on at Hyde Road until the summer of 1923 by which time their new stadium at Moss Side was ready. The last game at the ground, whose lease was up in any case, was a public practice match on 18th August 1923. City left straight after, taking with them just a few turnstiles and the goal posts. The remaining wooden stand not affected by the fire of 1920 was sold to Halifax Town for just under £1,000 and is still at The Shay.

Today, Hyde Road is the site of a bus depot, the actual pitch being covered with a skid pan for training in Bennett Street.

INTERNATIONAL PLAYERS

City's most-capped player (ie: caps gained while players were registered with the club) is Colin Bell with 48 caps. The following is a complete list of players who have gained full international honours while at Maine Road.

England	Caps	Wales	Caps
S.W. Austin	1	T. Chapman	1
S. Barkas	5	R.J. Clarke	22
P.S. Barnes	14	G. Davies	2
C. Bell	48	J. Davies	2
F. Booth	1	W.R. Davies	3
J. Bray	6	A. Dibble	1
I.A. Broadis	8	A. Gray	5
E.F. Brook	18	E. Hughes	3
H. Burgess	4	D. Jones	2
M.R. Channon	1	W.L. Jones	18
J.T. Corrigan	9	W. Lewis	2
S. Cowan	3	W.H. Meredith	22
K. Curle	3	H. Morris	1
M. Doyle	5	R. Paul	24
T.J. Francis	10	D.O. Phillips	10
T.C.F. Johnson	2	C.R. Sear	1
F.H. Lee	27	G.A. Wynn	8

England	Caps	Northern Ireland	Caps
R.W. Marsh	8	J.A. Crossan	10
J. Meadows	1	P. D. Doherty	6
J.F. Mitchell	1	G. Fleming	2
K.P. Reeves	1	M. Hamill	1
D.G. Revie	6	M.E. Hughes	4
F. Roberts	4	P. Kelly	1
J. Royle	4	S.M. Lomas	4
B. Sproston	1	W.J. McAdams	5
M.G. Summerbee	8	F.J. McCourt	6
F.V. Swift	19	K. McCullough	3
I. Thornley	1	S. McIlroy	10
F.S. Tilson	4	J. Mulligan	1
D. Tueart	6	M.H.M. O'Neill	1
D.V. Watson	30	W. Walsh	5
D. White	1		
M. Woosnam	1		
		Republic of Ireland	
Scotland		J.P. Conway	1
M.W. Busby	1	L. Dunne	2
W. Donachie	35	F. Fagan	2
A.R. Hartford	36	A. Kernaghan	4
R. Johnstone	4	M. McCarthy	20
D. Law	11	N. Quinn	30
G.T. Livingstone	1	T. Phelan	17
J.S. McLuckie	1	W. Walsh	9
J. McMullan	8		
J.B. Plenderleith	1	**Norway**	
G. Stewart	2	A. Hareide	9

City's first player to be capped was Joe Davies, who played for Wales against Ireland in 1890.

JOHNSON, TOM

Tom Johnson – "Tosh" to his colleagues and supporters – spent 11 seasons with Manchester City between 1919 and 1930 and scored a total of 166 league and cup goals for the club. In fact, he still holds the record for the club in the most goals in a single season. His 38 goals in 1928-29 in City's first season back in Division One, is the best-ever by a City player. He is also second in the club's list of all-time top goal-scorers in the League, being one behind Eric Brook.

It was City defender Eli Fletcher who insisted that the club sign Johnson from Dalton Casuals. Fletcher threatened not to re-sign unless the club moved in for the talented youngster who was performing wonders for his local club. Johnson signed and repaid City instantly, scoring on his debut in a Lancashire Section match before the League got underway after World War One. He made his league debut for City in February 1920, scoring twice against Middlesbrough.

He won two England caps, played in the 1926 FA Cup Final and helped City win promotion in 1927-28. In addition, he played for the Football League and FA XI. He was nearly 30 when City released him in March 1930, transferring him to Everton for £6,000. It wasn't the most popular of decisions and there were plenty of City supporters who criticised the club for letting him go and to underline their case they had to endure an outstanding performance by Johnson in the Everton side that defeated City in the 1933 FA Cup Final. In a successful career, he won three more caps for England whilst with Everton and collected First and Second Division championship medals.

JOHNSTONE, BOBBY

Born in Selkirk, Bobby Johnstone came to prominence with the Hibernian team of the immediate post-war era. Playing alongside such Scottish internationals as Gordon Smith, Osmond, Reilly and Turnbull, Johnstone soon made his name. In March 1955, City were induced to pay £22,000 for the versatile forward's signature and after Clarke and Hart were injured, the Blues' supporters had good reason to bless the men who brought the affable Scotsman to Maine Road.

Within 14 months of signing for City, Johnstone had become the first man to score in successive Wembley FA Cup Finals, his second effort helping the Blues to lift the trophy by beating Birmingham City 3-1.

Representing Scotland on 17 occasions, four of them with City, he also played for Great Britain against the Rest of Europe in August 1955, a few months after joining the Maine Road club. In September 1959, he returned to Hibs for £7,000 but within twelve months was back in Lancashire with Oldham Athletic.

JUNIOR BLUES CLUB

The Junior Blues Club was the first junior supporters' group formed by a Football League club and it has been the model on which many other similar organisations have been based.

Junior Blues' meetings are held regularly throughout the season at the City Social Club, Maine Road, usually on the third Sunday of the month, where players and club official attend to answer members' questions, sign autographs and play games. The club's President is Paul Lake.

KENDALL, HOWARD

Appointed Manchester City manager in December 1989, Howard Kendall won deserved accolades for keeping the club in the First Division and he oversaw a brilliant start to the 1990-91 season, but then angered City fans when he moved back to Everton. The draw was too great for Kendall, but the fans saw it as a lack of loyalty.

Kendall started his playing career at Preston North End and appeared in the 1964 FA Cup Final as a 17-year-old, the youngest-ever finalist at the time. In March 1967, he moved to Everton for £80,000 and soon won his first England Under-23 cap. Along with City's present manager Alan Ball and Colin Harvey, Kendall formed a brilliant midfield partnership that helped to bring the League Championship to Goodison in 1969-70. He later had spells at Birmingham City and Stoke City before becoming player-manager at Blackburn Rovers.

In just two years in charge at Ewood Park, he steered Rovers from a mid-table Third Division position to the brink of Division One.

In May 1981 he retired from playing and became manager of Everton. He was on the point of being sacked in January 1984 when the tide turned. Within six years he led Everton to two League Championships, the FA Cup and the European Cup-Winners' Cup.

He left for new challenges in Atletico Bilbao in 1987 before taking over at Maine Road halfway through the 1989-90 season. He made Peter Reid player-coach and brought in cult heroes like Tony Coton and Niall Quinn. Following his departure to Everton, Kendall's job was put on the line due to poor results in both the League and Cup competitions and he resigned.

City's full League record under Howard Kendall is:

P.	W.	D.	L.	F.	A.
32	12	15	5	39	30

KIPPAX STAND

From the moment it opened in August 1923, the large terracing opposite the Main Stand quickly became established as the "popular side" and in later years the Kippax.

In the early days the club's flagpole was positioned at the back of the terracing in line with the half-way line. On the morning of each game, a member of the City staff would raise the City flag and then when the game was over, lower it. Two large tunnels were built into the popular side – they allowed spectators to select their favourite position and helped to ensure that the club's huge crowds dispersed quickly and safely.

There was very little change to the popular side of the ground until the late 1950s when the decision was taken to spend some of the proceeds from the two successive FA Cup Finals on erecting a roof. The club announced that the new stand was to be officially known as the "Kippax Stand" and would hold around 32,000 under its new roof.

In the late sixties the City side were capable of beating anyone and the club's players became stars as the Kippax sang its way through the decade. In the seventies, with the seating of the North Stand in 1971, the Kippax became the club's last area of terracing and at the end of the decade, the official capacity was 26,155 out of an overall ground capacity of 52,600.

Over the last few years the capacity of the Kippax was reduced and when the final game of the 1993-94 season was played against Chelsea, the capacity was 18,300. The stand of course no longer exists, but nothing will ever take away the memories of its 71 year history.

LANCASHIRE COMBINATION

Before City's Reserve team played in the Central League, they played in the Lancashire Combination. Only once did they win the First Division, scoring 125 goals in 34 games in 1901-02. F. Bevan was the club's top-scorer and City's record that season was:

P.	W.	D.	L.	F.	A.
34	29	0	5	125	30

LANCASHIRE YOUTH CUP

The Lancashire Youth Cup began in 1972-73 when City became the first winners, beating neighbours Manchester United 5-0 over two legs in the final. In fact, City have won the trophy ten times since the competition began – more than any other club.

In the early eighties, the Blues won the cup in four consecutive seasons. The club's biggest win in the competition is 12-0 at Oldham Athletic in 1985-86, whilst three seasons later they won 11-1 at Bloomfield Road with Ward and Hasford scoring four goals apiece.

LARGEST CROWD

It was on 3rd March 1934 that Maine Road housed its largest crowd. The occasion was the FA Cup sixth round match against Stoke City. The crowd was a staggering 84, 569, also the highest for any match in Britain outside London or Glasgow. City won the match 1-0 with Eric Brook getting the goal.

LATE FINISHES TO A SEASON

City's latest finish to a league season was 14th June 1947 when George Smith scored all five goals in a 5-1 win over Newport County. During the war many curious things occurred and in 1940-41, City played their last match in the North Regional League against Bury on 7th June.

LEE, FRANCIS

Hailing from Westhoughton, Francis Lee made his league debut for Bolton Wanderers as a 16-year-old amateur in November 1960, after playing in only eight Central League games. He partnered 35-year-old Nat Lofthouse on the right-wing in a 3-1 victory over Manchester City. It was an eventful debut for the young star, Lee scoring a goal and getting booked.

He signed professional forms for the Wanderers in May 1961, but his volatile nature caused problems off the field when he refused to play after being dropped to the Bolton 'A' team. Things were patched up and though clubs were keen to sign him, following a string of transfer requests, Lee stayed with Bolton until the beginning of the 1967-68 season.

Moving to Maine Road in October 1967, he soon became a firm favourite with the City fans and was one of the successes in a team that enjoyed one of the greatest eras in the club's history.

Francis Lee, 1969

By the time he went to City, he was playing a more orthodox striking role. Lee was a bustling, sturdy, little striker. He had a barrel chest and though slightly portly, he was one of the most tenacious and effective of strikers, scoring many goals. He hit three hat-tricks in his years at Maine Road, including a spectacular threesome in the Manchester derby of 1970-71. His others came in the 5-2 thrashing of Wolverhampton Wanderers in January 1972 and in a 4-0 League Cup win over Walsall.

Francis Lee won a lot of penalties for City and wasn't really too fussy about how he won them. City won so many penalties during

1969: Willie McFaul saves from Tom Coleman and Francis Lee

the early seventies it became a topical talking point. In fact, many of them were awarded for fouls against Franny. In the European Cup Winners' Cup Final of 1970 against Gornik Zabrze of Poland, he hit the ball so hard and straight into the net, that it needed a close study of an action-replay to check the ball had not gone through Kostka, the goalkeeper's body!

In 1971-72, Lee topped the Division One goal-scorers with 33 goals including 15 from the penalty spot – a record! For this achievement he was awarded the bronze boot in the Golden Boot competition.

Lee was also a vital part of Sir Alf Ramsey's England squad and had gone to Mexico to defend the World Cup in 1970. In 27 appearances for England, he scored 10 goals.

In his 320 games for the Blues, he unleashed many devastating volleys, which led to a tally of 143 goals.

Moving to Derby County in August 1974 for £110,000, he won a second championship at the Baseball Ground before retiring in 1976.

By then his paper business which he started whilst a player with Bolton was a great success and eventually secured him millionaire status. Also, having obtained a licence in 1986, he became a breeder and trainer of racehorses near his Cheshire home. Becoming City Chairman in February 1994, Francis Lee is now concentrating his energies on building a successful future for Manchester City.

LONG SERVICE

Having a big hand in the club's early growth, Lawrence Furniss was with City for a total of 46 years. Helping to form the Ardwick Club, he joined the City board in 1903 until 1905, then rejoined in 1915 and was club chairman from 1921 to 1928. Later he was club president.

Wilf Wild was appointed City's assistant secretary in 1920 and secretary four years later, but in 1932 when manager Hodge returned to Leicester, Wild found himself in charge of team matters as well. He remained as manager until 1946 but when Sam Cowan was appointed in his place, he reverted to solely secretarial duties. He was still in office when he died in December 1950.

Les McDowall joined City from Sunderland in 1938 and made 129 first-team appearances until he moved to manage Wrexham in 1949. But in June 1950 he was appointed City manager, a position he held for 13 years.

Alan Oakes who made 669 first-team appearances after making his debut on 14th November 1959 gave almost 18 years service to the club. Other players include Joe Corrigan (1966-1983); Frank Swift (1932-1949) and Jackie Bray (1929-1946).

LOUGHBOROUGH TOWN

Loughborough Town spent five seasons all in the Second Division between 1895 and 1900, when they were not re-elected after finishing bottom of the table and winning just one game.

The two clubs met in four of those seasons, with City completing the double in three, including a 5-0 win on 17th December 1898 when Billy Meredith hit a hat-trick.

LOWEST

The lowest number of goals scored by Manchester City in a single Football League season is 36 in seasons 1949-50 and 1986-87 and on both occasions the club were relegated.

The Blues' lowest points total in the Football League occurred in 1893-94 when they gained just 18 points from a 28-match programme to finish thirteenth in the Second Division.

McDOWALL, LES

One of Manchester City's most distinguished and longest-serving managers, Les McDowall was born in India, the son of a Scottish missionary. McDowall trained as a draughtsman but was made unemployed from his shipyard in the early 1930s. Along with a number of others in the same position, they formed a football team, Glentyon Thistle and while playing for this side he was spotted by Sunderland and signed for them on Christmas Eve 1932. In over five years at Roker Park he was restricted to the occasional outing as deputy to skipper Alex Hastings or Scottish international centre-half Bert Johnstone. Although he made only 13 appearances for Sunderland, Manchester City were persuaded to pay £7,000 for his services in March 1938.

He took over the captaincy in 1938-39 but then the war disrupted his career. He returned to his draughtsman's job on the outbreak of hostilities, this time in an aircraft factory and played in wartime competitions for City. When League football resumed in 1946, McDowall was still a regular in the half-back line and although no longer captain, he helped them to the Second Division title in 1946-47.

In June 1949 he took over as manager of Wrexham. At the Racecourse Ground he selected himself just three times before hanging up his boots to concentrate on management. After less than a year at Wrexham, he was offered a return to City when manager Jock Thomson decided to leave football and run a hotel in his native Dundee. Just as his arrival as a player at Maine Road coincided with relegation to Division Two, so his ascension to manager in Manchester came as City dropped out of Division One. In his first season, he got them back to the top flight as runners-up and they remained there until the last of his 13 years at the helm. Relegation in 1963 led to McDowall's resignation and the end of his long association with City. He enjoyed a measure of success in the FA Cup and won a deserved reputation for tactical boldness and innovation. City reached Wembley in consecutive seasons, losing to Newcastle in 1955 and beating Birmingham in 1956. As a tactician, his major contribution was the so called "Revie Plan" which according to Revie himself could easily have been called the McDowall Plan. Although it started shakily, McDowall kept faith with the idea and it eventually paid off. To have lasted so long at Maine Road with little to show in terms of League honours suggests the confidence the club had in him.

Les McDowall

Les McDowall served the club well both as a player and manager. The loyalty he gave and was given is something that is sadly lacking in the modern game.

City's full League record under Les McDowall is:

P	W.	D.	L.	F.	A.
546	199	118	229	978	1064

McNEILL, BILLY

Billy could do no wrong in Scottish football. A commanding centre-half, he was a born leader. His decision to retire in 1975 brought to an end one of the most successful club careers of any British footballer. He made a traumatic debut for Scotland in the 9-3 defeat by England in 1961, but played in 831 games for Celtic which included their 1967 European Cup Final triumph. He collected 23 major winners' medals and in 1974 was awarded the M.B.E. for services to football.

He moved into management with Clyde in April 1977 but within two months he had moved to Aberdeen. The Dons narrowly missed out on the League title and the Scottish Cup and it was Billy who signed both Steve Archibald and Gordon Strachan for the Pittodrie club. In May 1978 he moved back to Parkhead, where he took over from Jock Stein. He stayed there for five years, winning more trophies before his move to Maine Road.

Billy took Manchester City to promotion to Division One in 1985 and to a Full Members' Cup Final appearance at Wembley where they lost 5-4 to Chelsea. In September 1986 he moved to take charge of Aston Villa, but at the end of the season they joined City in Division Two and Billy was sacked. After his dismissal he moved back to Parkhead to manage Celtic.

City's full League record under Billy is:

P.	W.	D.	L.	F.	A.
129	53	34	42	176	147

MACHIN, MEL

A cultured footballer, Mel Machin formed an effective and successful partnership with John Bond and followed him from Bournemouth to Norwich City. Machin helped the Canaries back into the First Division in 1975 and spent 14 years at Carrow Road before taking charge at Manchester City.

At Maine Road he put together a team that gained promotion in

Mel Machin

1989 while the books remained balanced. Under Machin, City played some very attractive and high-quality football. Machin managed City for one derby match only – a 5-1 win that was the best-ever derby win at home. After gaining promotion, City struggled in the First Division and Machin was sacked. He later managed Barnsley.

City's full League record under Mel Machin is:

P.	W.	D.	L.	F.	A.
104	46	23	35	174	148

MAINE ROAD

The club's new site at Maine Road was two miles west of Hyde Road and about three miles east of Old Trafford. Moss Side was densely populated but more important, the site offered the chance to build the biggest stadium in England apart from Wembley, which had just been completed.

One week after City's last game at Hyde Road on 25th August 1923, a crowd of 60,000 saw Lord Mayor, W. Cundiff pronounce Maine Road open, before City's opening First Division fixture against Sheffield United, which City won 2-1. on route to their second FA Cup triumph, City played Stoke City in the sixth round on 3rd March 1934. The attendance of 84,569 was the highest for any English club match apart from a Cup Final and the first of several attendance records Maine Road was to notch up.

After the war, Maine Road became the busiest ground in the country, for Old Trafford was unusable after extensive bomb damage and City played hosts to their neighbours. They could not have picked a better time to share the ground, because United were in top form in both League and Cup. This, allied to the spectacular rise in attendances following the war, meant that Maine Road was regularly packed to capacity.

In 1946-47, City won the Second Division championship, United were runners-up in the First Division, two representative matches were held at Maine Road, plus the Cup semi-final between Burnley and Liverpool and finally the ground also staged the Northern Rugby League Final. Altogether some 2,250,000 spectators had attended Maine Road in just one season, a record for any League ground.

By now attendances of over 70,000 were quite commonplace at Maine Road and in a short space of time in 1948 United attracted 82,950 for a match against Arsenal – the highest-ever League match attendance.

Maine Road therefore held the record attendances for both League and Cup matches. But even though City were charging United £5,000 a season plus a share of gate receipts in 1949 they asked United to leave.

Those post-war years brought in large profits and part of these were spent on an unusual development, the installation of seats on the Platt Lane terracing. It took Maine Road's seating capacity to about 18,500, more than any other club ground in Britain.

City were once more back in the First Division and on 14th October 1953 they switched on their floodlights for a friendly against Hearts. In 1956 City won the FA Cup for a third time and a huge roof was built over the Kippax Street banking opposite the Main Stand. This left only the North or Scoreboard End uncovered and meant that Maine Road was almost identical to Old Trafford for a spell during the 1960s.

New floodlights were installed in 1963-64 and a cantilever stand was built on the Scoreboard End with 8,120 seats.

In 1982 the Main Stand roof was again replaced at a cost of some £1 million which was paid for by the Supporters' Development Association. In 1994, the only area solely for standing spectators, the Kippax Street side was seated. The whole surrounds the largest football pitch in the English and Scottish Leagues and the club's under-soil heating has long been the envy of all Football League clubs. Sheltered within Maine Road is one of the friendliest clubs in the League. For while 35,000 packed the ground for a rock concert in 1986, over at the club's training ground on Platt Lane, a new sports centre financed jointly by the the club and an urban aid programme attracts over 60,000 people every year. No other League club has shown such a commitment to its local community.

MALEY, TOM

Tom Maley came from a footballing family of players, secretaries and managers, the most famous being his younger brother Willie, who was the manager of Celtic for many years.

He became secretary-manager at Hyde Road in July 1902 and in his first season in charge he steered the club to the Second Division title. In 1903-04, City beat Bolton Wanderers in the FA Cup Final and also finished runners-up in the First Division. Maley liked the Scottish style of play, which was a skilful, close-passing game. He signed Livingstone and Burgess, a couple of useful players to enhance a squad which already included Billy Meredith and Sandy Turnbull.

Alas, in 1906, Maley became embroiled in the scandal over illegal payments at the club and was suspended *sine die* along with City chairman W. Forrest. Many of the players were also fined and suspended for shorter periods. For Manchester City it was the end of a great era and with it went the man largely responsible, Tom Maley. In 1911, the FA decided to end Maley's suspension and he became the manager of Bradford. He later had a short period in charge of Southport before leaving the game for good.

City's full League record under Tom Maley is:

P.	W.	D.	L.	F.	A.
140	83	21	36	305	165

MANAGERS

Overleaf is the complete list of City's full-time managers with the inclusive dates in which they held office. Biographies of these managers are included in alphabetical order in this A-Z.

Lawrence Furniss	1889-1893	Malcolm Allison	1972-1973
Joshua Parlby	1893-1895	Johnny Hart	1973
Sam Ormerod	1895-1902	Ron Saunders	1973-1974
Tom Maley	1902-1906	Tony Book	1974-1979
Harry Newbould	1906-1912	Malcolm Allison	1979-1980
Ernest Mangnall	1912-1924	John Bond	1980-1983
David Ashworth	1924-1925	John Benson	1983
Peter Hodge	1926-1932	Billy Billy	1983-1986
Wilf Wild	1932-1946	Jimmy Frizzell	1986-1987
Sam Cowan	1946-1947	Mel Machin	1987-1989
Jock Thomson	1947-1950	Howard Kendall	1989-1990
Les McDowall	1950-1963	Peter Reid	1990-1993
George Poyser	1963-1965	Brian Horton	1993-1995
Joe Mercer	1965-1971	Alan Ball	1995-

MANCHESTER UNITED

Regardless of the triumphs or disasters of a particular season, the derby clash with Manchester United has always been the most important fixture in both clubs' footballing calendar. Although there had been many games between Newton Heath (United) and Ardwick (City) and an FA Cup tie in 1891, the first League encounter occurred in 1894 when both teams were in the Second Division. These early derbies revolved around the ambition to join the First Division, where Newton Heath had played between 1892-94. Despite United's pre-eminence in these early matches (City only won two of the first 10 derbies) it was the Blues who gained promotion at the end of the 1898-99 season. City's 4-0 thrashing of their neighbours proved the conclusive spur on the road to promotion.

In the First Division, both teams set out to win the game's major honours. It was United who dominated not only the derby, but English football winning the Championship twice and the Cup once between 1907 and 1911.

City's powerful inside-forward Horace Barnes made the 33rd derby in October 1921 memorable by scoring the first hat-trick since the inaugural match as City trounced a poor United side 4-1. In January 1926 City were having a dreadful time with only six wins in 25 outings and a comfortable home win for United seemed a certainty. What transpired was the record derby victory over six goals to one, achieved by the men from Maine Road. In fact, it was City that had the better of contests in the inter-war years.

The emergence of former City player, Matt Busby in the manager's job at Old Trafford in 1945, galvanised the club almost immediately, making them a major power in the post-war game. The 78,000 crowd that attended the first post-war City-United derby clash in September 1947 set the derby attendance record that is now likely to stand forever.

Two late goals by United's Stan Pearson in September 1949 foiled the Blues of likely victory and led to the unprecedented scene of the gentlemanly Frank Swift chasing the referee half the length of the pitch to protest over the first goal. In 1954-55 City narrowly won the season's first derby at Maine Road by the odd goal in five. Hart's winner was the perfect example of the "Revie Plan" as he ghosted into the centre-forwards space vacated by the deep-lying Revie to shoot past Ray Wood. The fourth round of that season's FA Cup paired the two teams again, with City winning 2-0 and Revie scoring the second goal. In the return league fixture at Old Trafford, City equalled the margin of their record 1926 victory, silencing the home crowd with a stunning 5-0 victory. The derbies following the Munich Air Disaster were poor affairs, not surprisingly inhibited by the glories of yester-year.

By the end of the 1962-63 season, City and United were both involved in a desperate battle to stay in the First Division. The match that was to determine which of the two Manchester clubs would face the drop was played on 15th May 1963 in front of 52,424 crowd at Maine Road. Alex Harley gave the Blues an early lead but a late Albert Quixall penalty banished City to the Second Division, where they would stay for three seasons.

But by 1968, Manchester could be claimed to be England's soccer capital, with the United of Best, Law and Charlton neck-and-neck for the title with the City of Bell, Lee and Summerbee. Once again the derby contest had a vital influence on the outcome. Old Trafford erupted after 35 seconds to salute a brilliant George Best goal, but City bounced back to secure a famous victory with goals courtesy of Heslop, Lee and Bell. It was a crucial result in the Championship race, since City did indeed win the title with just two more points than nearest rivals United.

The Reds had to endure some crushing defeats – none worse than Christmas 1970 when Francis Lee scored a hat-trick as City won 4-1 in front of a despondent Old Trafford crowd.

In 1974 Tommy Docherty's side had to score a home victory in the penultimate game of the season to have any chance of escape in the final fixture. A draw seemed the likely outcome until in one of the most famous moments in the history of the derby, the game was settled. Denis Law received the ball on the United penalty spot from a Lee pass and instinctively back-heeled the ball past a startled Alex Stepney and into the net, plunging the crowd into silence and sealing his former club's fate.

In September 1989 few of the fans who turned up at Maine Road expected anything other than a United victory. What transpired was a 5-1 City win which equalled their best-ever home performance in the history of the fixture. last season of course, United won 5-0 and 3-0 but this contest remains as important and unpredictable today as it was over a century ago.

MANGNALL, ERNEST

Ernest Mangnall was the first great manager of Manchester United, helping them to two League Championships and an FA Cup success. Born in Bolton, he had kept goal for the Lancashire County side, won road races as a cyclist and was a good cross-country runner who represented Bolton Harriers.

At United, Mangnall developed the ability to motivate players and was also able to spot talent and develop it. It was Mangnall who signed Sandy Turnbull and Billy Meredith from City when they were hit by an illegal payments scandal.

In August 1912, Mangnall surprisingly left United to manage Manchester City. It was a difficult period for the Hyde Road club, but he managed to keep them in the First Division and then kept them going through the rigours of wartime football. City finished fifth in 1914-15 and runners-up in 1920-21. They also reached the semi-finals of the FA Cup in 1924 but lost 2-0 to Newcastle United. In May 1924 his contract was not renewed and he left the club two months later.

A founder of the Central League and the man largely responsible for the formation of the Football Managers' Association, he was awarded a long-service medal by the FA in 1921 after 21 years service to football.

City's full League record under Ernest Mangnall is:

P	W.	D.	L.	F.	A.
324	139	76	109	463	431

MARATHON MATCH

It was in the 1905-06 season that Manchester City and Bolton Wanderers to decide a single tie the Manchester Senior Cup, played each other in four matches. The first three matches were all drawn 1-1 before Bolton won the fourth by the only goal of the game. Before the issue was decided, the two clubs had actually played for seven hours!

MARSHALL, BOB

A native of Hucknall in Nottinghamshire, Bob Marshall's first club was Sunderland, for whom he made almost 200 league appearances. Joining Manchester City in March 1928, he went on to become an important member of a fine City team, appearing in consecutive FA Cup Finals and gaining a winners' medal in 1934. In these early years with the Blues he starred as an inside-forward who not only possessed brilliant ball-control, he could also find his way to goal. After City's success over Portsmouth in that 1934 Final, he received a £650 benefit and after converting to centre-half in an emergency, he began a 'second career'. It was a career that saw him perform wonders in the City defence that helped win the League Championship in 1936-37.

After making 355 first-team appearances for City he transferred to Stockport County in March 1939. He later managed Stockport as well as Chesterfield.

MERCER, JOE

One of the game's all-time greats, Joe Mercer had a great career both as a player and a manager. He began his career as a junior with

Everton in 1932 and stayed with them until 1946. In that time he developed into one of the finest wing-halves in the country and helped the Toffees to the League Championship in 1938-39 when war came. He lost seven seasons of top-class soccer but played regularly in wartime soccer, being part of a famous England half-back line with Cullis and Cliff Britton. Out of favour with Everton he moved to Arsenal where his career was rejuvenated. He led the Gunners first clear of relegation, then to the League Championship in 1947-48 as cap-

Joe Mercer, 1967

tain. He played in his first FA Cup Final for the club in 1950 when they beat Liverpool; two seasons later they lost to Newcastle United in the Final. Mercer was voted Footballer of the Year in 1950 a..d gained another League championship medal in 1952-53. His illustrious career came to an end when he broke his leg in April 1954 against Blackpool at Highbury, just before his 40th birthday.

Mercer went into management first with Sheffield United and then Aston Villa. At Villa Park he saw the club promoted from the Second Division, reach two FA Cup semi-finals and win the League Cup. However, in 1964, Mercer suffered a stroke due to over-work. The Villa directors waited until he was over the worst effects, then sacked him.

Most people thought his retirement was permanent, but in July 1965, he made a come-back as manager of Manchester City. Along with his assistant, Malcolm Allison, Mercer revitalised a club that had been in the doldrums for far too long. City won the Second Division title in 1965-66, then the League Championship two years later. More trophies soon followed as City beat Leicester to take the 1969 FA Cup Final and then the European Cup-Winners' Cup the following year.

In June 1972, Mercer moved to become general manager at Coventry City and in 1974 took temporary charge of the England team. Mercer was awarded an O.B.E. for his services to football in 1976. In 1981 he resigned from the Coventry board after six years as a director at Highfield Road. After this, Mercer lived in retirement on Merseyside, until his death in August 1990.

City's full League record under Joe Mercer is:

P.	W.	D.	L.	F.	A.
294	126	85	83	448	329

MEREDITH, BILLY

Billy Meredith was a phenomenon, a footballing freak, an ageing genius who refused to grow old and who, well into his forties was still able to make full-backs wish they had never been born.

His figures are staggering. He played top-class football for no less than 30 years, from 1894 when at 19, he joined Manchester City from Chirk, his home town just across the Shropshire-Wales border, to 1924, when he was accepted for every Cup-tie in City's run to the semi-final. He played 367 league games for City and another 303, almost a career in itself for Manchester United between 1906 and 1921. He scored 181 League and 56 Cup goals.

His international record is equally impressive. In the days when Wales' opponents were limited to England, Scotland and Ireland, he was selected for 71 consecutive matches between 1895 and 1920 but, because of the demands of his clubs (particularly City!) he was released for only 48 of them, plus the three victory internationals in 1919.

Tall, gaunt and shambling, almost casual in appearance, he became

Billy Meredith

transformed with a ball at his feet. His runs to the corner flag and the devastating cross might be varied by his sudden cut inside – he was as fast as he was skilful – for a shot at goal. When faced with a blanket of close-marking defenders, as he so often was, Meredith's answer was as unexpected as it was brilliant. With a jink of his tall frame he would lean right in to the would-be-tackler, then accelerate past him; the tackler would give chase only to find that Meredith had, with his jink, flicked a back pass to his own right-half, drawn off all the defenders and left the field open for attack.

As celebrated as the shot and the back-pass were the toothpick and the penalty. The first rolling ceaselessly from one side of his mouth to the other throughout his career was a unique trademark – all the more so, perhaps, for the fact that he never once swallowed one! The penalty was a piece of inspired and effective clowning. At the turn of the century a goalkeeper could advance to the six-yard box and Meredith was a master of looping the ball over his head.

Meredith's relationships with his two clubs were not as serene as his long service would suggest. He appears to have been an outspoken and headstrong young man, furious at his club's frequent refusals to release him to play for Wales and disgusted with the miserable wages. It was money that led to his move to United in 1906, two years after he had scored the goal that gave City the FA Cup. Eighteen City players, Meredith among them were suspended for receiving "illegal payments", that is 5s and 10s bonuses. Immediately after the suspension he moved to United and, within three seasons had won League and Cup medals with his new club. In 1921 a free-transfer saw him back with City.

His return match was against Aston Villa, played at City's ground in Hyde Road. Meredith performed with much of his old audacity, delighting a crowd of 35,000. Villa were beaten 2-1 and the veteran Welshman played a large part in the scoring of the first City goal.

A further two years later the Welsh Wizard was called up to the City squad for the third round FA Cup tie against Brighton and he played in the three subsequent ties. The semi-final against Newcastle United was Billy Meredith's last game for City. On 25th April 1925, over 15,000 people attended Maine Road for Billy Meredith's testimonial. That day a team of his own choosing played a combined Celtic and Rangers XI. The game, a 2-2 draw, was played with such panache that it was totally worthy of Meredith's achievements.

MIDDLESBROUGH IRONOPOLIS

They spent just one season in the League, 1893-94 and finished eleventh in the Second Division. City beat them 6-1 at Hyde Road but lost 2-0 in the return fixture.

MOST GOALS IN A SEASON

Manchester City scored 108 goals in forty-two Division Two matches during the 1926-27 season. They scored in every home game and only failed to score in three away fixtures. Sixty-five goals came at home and in eleven games, four or more goals were scored. At Maine Road, Bradford City were beaten 8-0, Darlington 7-0 and Clapton Orient 6-1. The top scorer was Tommy Johnson with 25 goals, whilst Hicks had 21. City finished the season in third place.

MOST MATCHES

The most first-class matches played by City in a single season is 60 in 1969-70. This figure includes nine European Cup-Winners' Cup, two FA Cup and seven Football League Cup fixtures along with 42 Division One matches.

In the space of four weeks in April 1904, City played 11 matches:

Date	Opponents	Competition	Venue	Score
01.04.1904	Newcastle United	Division 1	Home	1-3
02.04.1904	Sunderland	Division 1	Home	2-1
04.04.1904	Manchester United	Man Sen Cup	Home	1-1
07.04.1904	Manchester United	Man Sen Cup	Away	2-1
09.04.1904	West Brom Albion	Division 1	Away	1-2
11.04.1904	Bury	Division 1	Home	3-0
13.04.1904	Notts Forest	Division 1	Home	0-0
16.04.1904	Small Heath	Division 1	Home	4-0
23.04.1904	Bolton Wanderers	FA Cup Final	Neutral	1-0
25.04.1904	Everton	Division 1	Away	0-1
30.04.1904	Bury	Man Sen Cup	Home	0-0

NEUTRAL GROUNDS

Maine Road has been used as a neutral ground for FA Cup matches on a number of occasions and in 1938 staged an international match between England and Northern Ireland. In 1946 the ground was used for England v Scotland, a match played in aid of the Bolton Disaster Fund and England v Wales.

The ground was awarded a semi-final replay between Huddersfield Town and Sheffield United on 2nd April 1928, the first of many such occasions. In 1950, Maine Road was the venue of the Liverpool v Everton FA Cup semi-final which the Reds won. Everton meanwhile were back three years later only to lose 4-3 to Bolton Wanderers, who at one stage were four goals up. The men from Burnden Park returned in 1958 to defeat Blackburn Rovers 2-1 in the same stage of the competition.

Maine Road has also been the venue for a Milk Cup Final replay, an FA Amateur Cup Final replay and numerous England Under-21 matches. Manchester City themselves have had to replay on a neutral ground a number of times.

Date	Opponents	Venue	FA Cup	Score
16.03.1914	Sheffield United	Villa Park	Round 4	0-1
11.02.1924	Halifax Town	Old Trafford	Round 2	3-0
16.01.1961	Cardiff City	Highbury	Round 3	2-0
05.04.1966	Everton	Molineux	Round 6	0-2

Date	Opponents	Venue	FLg Cup	Score
30.10.1973	Walsall	Old Trafford	Round 2	4-0
24.09.1975	Norwich City	Stamford Br	Round 2	6-1
09.11.1977	Luton Town	Old Trafford	Round 3	3-2

The club's semi-finals were, of course, played on neutral grounds.

Date	Opponents	Venue	Score
19.03.1904	Sheffield Wednesday	Goodison Park	3-1
29.03.1924	Newcastle United	St Andrews	0-2
27.03.1926	Manchester United	Bramall Lane	3-0
12.03.1932	Arsenal	Villa Park	0-1
18.03.1933	Derby County	Leeds Road	3-2
17.03.1934	Aston Villa	Leeds Road	6-1
26.03.1955	Sunderland	Villa Park	1-0
17.03.1956	Tottenham Hotspur	Villa Park	1-0
22.03.1969	Everton	Villa Park	1-0
11.04.1981	Ipswich Town	Villa Park	1-0

The club's appearances in the Full Members' Cup Final v Chelsea (at Wembley on 23rd March 1986) and the European Cup-Winners' Cup Final v Gornik Zabrze (at Vienna on 29th April 1970) and the third round replay against the same opposition in Copenhagen on 31st March 1971 also qualify, as do the club's numerous FA Cup and Football League Cup Finals at The Crystal Palace and Wembley.

NEWBOULD, HARRY

Harry Newbould was born in the Everton district of Liverpool and never played professional football. Instead he appeared for Derby St Lukes, a leading local side and made a name for himself as a sprinter. A qualified accountant, Newbould was appointed as assistant-secretary at Derby in 1896 and later promoted to secretary. In 1900 he was appointed as Derby County's first secretary-manager. A popular figure, he brought many fine players to the club, although he sold the highly successful Steve Bloomer to Middlesbrough – to the dismay of Derby supporters.

In July 1906 Newbould surprised and disappointed the Derby board by becoming secretary-manager of Manchester City. The prospects at City looked very bleak. They had just lost most of their playing staff after a financial scandal at the club over illegal payments to players had led to a number of suspensions. Newbould had to completely rebuild the team, but this took time and City had a disastrous start to the season, losing their first two league games of 1906-07, 4-1 and 9-1. But after a number of shrewd signings, City began to improve and in 1907-08, finished third in Division One. The following season though they were relegated but bounced back as champions of the Second Division in 1909-10. There followed another struggle against relegation in 1911-12 – only a late run of 17 points from ten games saw City to safety – before Newbould ended his days at Hyde Road.

Not lost to football administration, he ended his days as secretary of the Players' Union, the forerunner of today's PFA. City's full League record under Harry Newbould is:

P.	W.	D.	L.	F.	A.
228	86	57	85	362	356

NEW BRIGHTON

After finishing fourth in the Second Division they resigned in 1900-01 after three seasons in the League, all in the Second Division. A re-formed club joined the League in 1923.

City played them in 1898-99, drawing 1-1 on the Wirral and winning 1-0 at home thanks to a Billy Gillespie goal.

NEWPORT COUNTY

Newport County played more matches than any other ex-member of the Football League. In the 61 seasons after they joined the newly formed Third Division in 1920, they played 2,672 games. Champions of the Third Division (South) in 1938-39, they spent just one season in Division Two and that was on the resumption of the Football League in 1946-47 and when they met City. The Blues won 3-0 at Newport and completed the double over their Welsh counterparts in the final game of the season, winning 5-1 at Maine Road with George Smith scoring all five of City's goals.

They lost their league place automatically after finishing bottom of the Fourth Division in 1987-88.

NICKNAMES

Many players in the club's history have been fondly known to supporters by their nicknames.

Known as "The Doc", William Holmes was a big, strong half-back whose fearsome tackles made him a most feared opponent. After being left out of City's 1904 FA Cup Final team, he threw his boots through the dressing-room window!

Frank Booth was nicknamed "Tabby" and served the club well in the early part of the century. Playing on the opposite flank to Billy Meredith, he was adept at swinging over a succession of precise crosses for his colleagues to capitalise on.

Tommy Browell was known as "Boy" after scoring a hat-trick for Hull City against Stockport in October 1910 when just 18 years of age. He later signed for City and went on to score 139 goals in 247 first-team appearances.

Invariably known as "Spud" Bill Murphy was a speedy outside-left renowned for his quickness. The story goes that local pigeon fanciers paid him to convey the birds' arrival times to headquarters!

Known as "Buzzer", Mike Summerbee was a traditional outside-right, but as his career with City began to unfold, he assumed a much more versatile role and shared in City's rise to success. Alongside him was Colin Bell, nicknamed "Nijinsky" after the racehorse. His enthusiasm and boundless energy made him one of the most influential players of his day. He played in almost 500 competitive games for City and gained winners' medals for the League Championship, FA Cup. League Cup and European Cup-Winners' Cup.

NON-LEAGUE

"Non-League" is the shorthand term for clubs which are not members of the Football League. Manchester City do not have a particularly good record against non-league clubs in the FA Cup competition, though they did beat their last opponents, Wigan Athletic in 1970-71.

The club's record is:

Date	Opponents	Venue	Score
22.09.1892	Fleetwood Rangers	Away	1-1
05.10.1892	Fleetwood Rangers	Home	0-2
14.10.1893	West Manchester	Away	0-3
29.01.1897	Wigan County	Home	1-0
02.01.1970	Wigan Athletic	Home	1-0

NORTHWICH VICTORIA

Like City, a founder member of the Second Division in 1892-93, they resigned after two seasons. of their four encounters, City won three and drew one, completing the double in 1893-94, when they won 4-2 at home and 4-1 away.

OAKES, ALAN

Alan Oakes never played any organised football until he left junior school to attend Winsford Secondary Modern. He left school at 15 after representing mid-Cheshire boys and immediately joined Manchester City. He had always played at inside-forward in school football, but had a number of games at wing-half for the county side and it was this position he adopted when he joined City.

He made his first-team debut on 14th November 1959 against Chelsea as a stand-in for the injured Ken Barnes. In his debut season, he had to help City fight against relegation which was avoided only in the fortieth match when Colin Barlow's goal secured victory over Preston North End.

Alan Oakes, 1967

It was towards the end of the following season that Ken Barnes retired from the first-class game and Oakes was in! His early years at Maine Road in the first half of the 1960s were spent in a poor City side. However, Oakes held on and was rewarded with plenty of honours in the remainder of his career with City. He won a Second Division championship medal, followed by a First Division championship medal, two League Cup winners' medals, an FA Cup winners' medal and a European Cup-winners' Cup medal. He didn't manage to acquire a full England cap but he did play for the Football League against the Scottish League at Hampden Park in March 1969. over the two seasons prior to this, he had been chosen for the full England squad on three occasions, but still awaited that elusive first cap. There have certainly been more flamboyant footballers than Alan Oakes who have won England caps, but certainly not as talented. He was a player who made great surging runs from midfield, Young and Coleman in particular benefiting. Despite playing at wing-half, he was always fortunate enough to score a number of goals for City. Against Atletico Bilbao in the second leg of the Cup-Winners' match at Maine Road, after the first leg in Spain had been drawn at 3-3, he let fly from fully 30 yards as the Spanish defence backed off and the ball rocketed into the net. Swindon Town were the opponents and when Mike Summerbee (not yet with City) threw the ball to a surprised Oakes, he killed it, swung round and hit it terrifically hard from 40 yards with his left foot to score.

Alan Oakes was a quiet, gentle, unassuming player – a player who got on with the job without any fuss. He was rewarded with a testimonial against Manchester United in 1972. To mark his 500th appearance he was presented with a silver salver before the game against Stoke City on 9th November 1974.

In July 1976, having helped City to yet another success at Wembley, he signed for Chester for a fee of £15,000, later becoming player-manager. His part in the history of Manchester City Football Club cannot be over-estimated. He played in 669 games for City – more than any other player.

ORMEROD, SAM

Sam Ormerod was Manchester City's first secretary-manager, but he did not have sole charge in his seven years at the club, during which City were promoted and relegated.

He gained a reputation as a player and referee in local Lancashire soccer in the 1880s. He officially became City's manager in 1895, as part of a three-man committee which included his predecessor Joshua Parlby. Ormerod exerted the biggest influence on the committee and helped spot many fine players for the club. Ormerod had little tactical awareness and many of the problems that he encountered were because of this. His main role was to select the team. City finished runners-up in 1895-96 and qualified for the Test Matches, although they did not do very well in these. They finished sixth and third in the next two seasons, then became champions of Division Two in

1898-99. City found the going tough in the First Division and at the end of 1901-02 were relegated.

Ormerod resigned in July 1902 after receiving a lot of criticism on how the club was being run financially by those attending a share-holders' meeting. They were especially critical of the amount being spent on travelling, expenses, bonuses and wages. Unfortunate to have been City manager when the club were still thinking in parochial terms, he did after all help to lay the foundations of the team which won the FA Cup for the first time in the club's history.

City's full League record under Sam Ormerod is:

P.	W.	D.	L.	F.	A.
226	108	47	71	419	319

OVERSEAS TOURS

City's first ever tour was in May 1910 when they visited Germany, Denmark and Sweden. There was then a twenty-two year gap before the Blues toured France, winning all three fixtures.

After the war, the club became a little more adventurous and toured North America, Australia, South Africa and the Far East.

On all of their travels, the club have hit double figures on five occasions:

v Aarhus, Denmark	11-1	18th May 1938
v IFK Rundvik, Sweden	10-0	25th July 1988
v Lovangers AIK, Sweden	12-0	26th July 1988
v Lervik, Norway	10-0	29th July 1990
v Skelleften AIK, Sweden	11-1	27th July 1991

OWN GOALS

Dave Ewing holds the unenviable record of the most post-war own goals for Manchester City with ten – nine in the league and one in the FA Cup. However, many of his misfortunes came into the "unlucky" category of own goals – the result of desperate last-ditch clearances in situations where the Blues were totally overrun.

Scottish centre-half John McTavish achieved three own-goals in four league games in November 1959, the lucky recipients being West Ham, West Brom and Newcastle. Three times since the war a City player has scored for both sides in a game. The first was Derek Kevan in a 4-3 defeat at Charlton in February 1964. The second was Steve Mackenzie in a 2-2 draw at Middlesbrough in August 1980 and the third and one of the unluckiest players to score at both ends – was Tommy Hutchison the 1981 Centenary FA Cup Final against Tottenham Hotspur. He was the first player to achieve this in a Final since 1946.

Perhaps one of the most bizarre own-goals was the one by Dave Watson against Liverpool on an icy Maine Road pitch in December 1976. If City had won, they would have gone joint-top of the First Division with the Reds. City were leading 1-0 with just two minutes left when Watson sank to his knees and skilfully headed the ball to where he thought Corrigan was. But Joe was no longer there, having come for the cross!

One of the funniest own-goals came in Bert Trautmann's Testimonial match. A combined City and United XI faced an International XI before a crowd of almost 48,000. Within a few minutes, United's Maurice Setters in unfamiliar sky-blue blasted a shot past a bemused Trautmann and began to dance for joy. He said later "I've always wanted to score against Bert and tonight was going to be my last chance. I couldn't resist it!"

PARDOE, GLYN

The cousin of Alan Oakes, Glyn Pardoe was only 15 years 314 days old when he made his league debut for City against Birmingham on 11th April 1962. He kept his place for a further three games before being rested, but it was obvious that young Glyn had potential.

What was not yet apparent was his best position. As a schoolboy, he had played centre-half for his school team but was converted to centre-forward by the England Boys manager and against Wales in 1960-61, scored four goals.

For City in 1963-64 he played in a variety of positions and it wasn't until Mercer and Allison arrived that he turned out at left-back, a position he was to keep for some years to come.

Glyn Pardoe, 1967

In 1967-68 he won four England Under-23 caps as City won the League Championship for the second time in their history. He even got on the score sheet in the 1970 League Cup Final, hitting home the winning goal in extra-time as City beat West Bromwich Albion 2-1.

Then, he broke a leg in the Mancunian derby game on 12th December 1970. Not only did Glyn almost lose his leg, which had five fractures and a trapped main artery but his life was also in danger and it was the speed and skill of the surgeons that saved him.

Apart from 1973-74 when he made 31 League appearances, he never regained a regular place. He joined the club's coaching staff, working with reserves and juniors for ten years. A loyal servant of the club, he not only won many honours, but also did a valuable job in bringing on the younger players.

PARLBY, JOSHUA

Joshua Parlby had played for Stoke before becoming a member of that club's committee. In 1893 he became City's first paid secretary, but they were traumatic days for the club, Bankruptcy and a crippling defection of first-team players in September 1894 nearly finished them off. The club re-emerged as Manchester City and managed to retain their place in the Football League, thanks largely to the work of Joshua Parlby. There is a story that he smuggled the hard-up City team up and down the railway system when they could not afford to travel legitimately to fulfil their fixtures.

A gifted amateur, Parlby knew very little about football tactics, but a burly boisterous man, he excelled in the art of wrangling. He signed Billy Meredith before taking over a public house in Bolton in 1895. He also joined the City board from then until 1905. He rejoined the board in April 1909 and served for a further three years, when he retired and left the area.

City's full League record under Joshua Parlby is:

P.	W.	D.	L.	F.	A.
58	22	5	31	129	143

PAUL, ROY

A native of the Rhondda, Roy Paul was an ex-coal miner who joined City from Swansea Town in July 1950 for £25,000. A regular throughout his Maine Road career, he made 293 League and Cup appearances for the club in only seven seasons.

His first taste of senior soccer came in 1939 in a wartime League game for Swansea and when football resumed after the hostilities, he was a member of the Vetch Field's side which won the Third Division (South) title.

Paul also looked with interest at the situation in Colombia, when other British players like Neil Franklin and Charlie Mitten went to Bogota in search of soccer fortune, but decided to stay in Britain and join City. When the Blues won promotion to the First Division in 1950-51, Paul was a star performer, missing only one game and scoring three goals. Two of them came in the 3-1 win at home to Birmingham City on Christmas Day 1950. Some six years later, he captained Manchester City to success in the FA Cup Final in another 3-1 victory over the Midlands side, twelve months after he had collected a losers' medal against Newcastle United. Winning 33 Welsh caps, 24 of them whilst he was with City, he joined Worcester City in June 1957 as their player-manager.

PENALTIES

City chairman Francis Lee holds the club's overall penalty scoring record. He netted a total of 46 in his career with City in competitive games.

On 27th January 1912, City missed three penalties in one game. This was at Newcastle, the culprits being Eli Fletcher (2) and Irvine Thornley. The game ending level at 1-1. Newcastle were City's opponents in the last game of the 1925-26 season when the Blues travelled north to St James' Park. Hoping to register their fifth consecutive win, they needed one point to avoid relegation but Billy Austin missed a penalty, City lost 3-2 and went down!

On 7th December 1957, Ken Barnes, the father of Peter Barnes, scored a hat-trick of penalties when City beat Everton 6-2 at Maine Road. For good measure he scored one in the return fixture at Goodison Park.

In April 1991, City beat Derby County 2-1. Doomed to play Second Division soccer the following season, the Rams seemed certain to score from the spot when Coton had been sent off for dragging down Dean Saunders. Into the nets went Niall Quinn. Having scored at the other end, he made history when he saved Dean Saunders' penalty!

PLASTIC

There have been four Football League clubs that have replaced their normal grass playing pitches with artificial surfaces at one stage or another. Queen's Park Rangers were the first in 1981, but the Loftus Road pitch was discarded in 1988 in favour of a return to turf. Luton Town (1985), Oldham Athletic (1986) and Preston North End (1986) followed.

City have never played on the Deepdale plastic. They visited the Loftus Road plastic on two occasions, drawing 0-0 in 1985-86 and losing 1-0 the following season. City visited Kenilworth Road, the home of Luton Town on four occasions, drawing two and losing two. They played Oldham Athletic for the first time in 1987-88 and drew 1-1 before winning at Boundary Park the following season 1-0, courtesy of a Gary Megson goal – City's only win in eight matches on plastic!

PLAYER OF THE YEAR

The award by Manchester City supporters dates from season 1966-67
and the winners have been as follows:

1966-67	Tony Book	1981-82	Tommy Caton
1967-68	Colin Bell	1982-83	Kevin Bond
1968-69	Glyn Pardoe	1983-84	Mick McCarthy
1969-70	Francis Lee	1984-85	Paul Power
1970-71	Mike Doyle	1985-86	Kenny Clements
1971-72	Mike Summerbee	1986-87	Neil McNab
1972-73	Mike Summerbee	1987-88	Steve Redmond
1973-74	Mike Doyle	1988-89	Neil McNab
1974-75	Alan Oakes	1989-90	Colin Hendry
1975-76	Joe Corrigan	1990-91	Niall Quinn
1976-77	Dave Watson	1991-92	Tony Coton
1977-78	Joe Corrigan	1992-93	Gary Flitcroft
1978-79	Asa Hartford	1993-94	Tony Coton
1979-80	Joe Corrigan	1994-95	Uwe Rosler
1980-81	Paul Power		

*Steve Redmond in action against Rick Holden of Oldham Athletic, to which he
transferred after the 1992/93 season*

POINTS

Under the three points for a win system, which was introduced in 1981-82, City's best points tally was the 82 points in 1988-89, when the club gained promotion from the Second Division. However, the club's best points haul under the old two points for a win system was 62 points in the Second Division championship-winning season of 1946-47, which would have netted them 86 points under the present method.

The club's worst record under either system was the meagre 18 points secured in 1893-94, though that was from a 28-match programme. The lowest points total from a 42-match programme is 31 which City managed in 1958-59 and 1962-63 when they were relegated.

POSTPONED

City's opening game of the 1957-58 season against Sheffield Wednesday was postponed due to an outbreak of influenza at Hillsborough. When the game was rearranged, City beat the Owls 2-0 with goals from Barlow and McAdams.

POWER, PAUL

Discovered by Harry Godwin, Paul Power was a student at Leeds Polytechnic when he was turning out for City Reserves in the Central League. Signing professional forms in July 1975, he made his league debut the following month at Villa Park. Not a prolific goal-scorer, he opened his City account with the winner in a thrilling match against Derby County which City won 4-3.

In October 1979, Malcolm Allison handed Power the club captaincy and he celebrated by leading the Blues to a surprise 1-0 win over Nottingham Forest. The majority of Paul Power's career at Maine Road was spent on the left side of midfield, though he was also played at left-back.

In 1981 he scored from a free-kick in the FA Cup semi-final defeat

Paul Power, 1982

of Ipswich Town, but couldn't repeat the feat in the Wembley final against Tottenham Hotspur. Power's second appearance at the Twin Towers with City came in the 1986 Full Members' Cup Final when the Blues lost 5-4 to Chelsea. His one and only representative honour came in 1981 with an appearance in the England v Spain 'B' international.

In June 1986, Howard Kendall took him away from Maine Road and gave him a place in Everton's League Championship side. He had appeared in 445 first-team games for City and scored 36 goals. Power later moved on to the coaching staff at Goodison Park.

POYSER, GEORGE

George Poyser made a name for himself as a full-back with Port Vale before moving to Brentford in 1934. In his first season with the club he was an ever-present as they clinched the Second Division championship.

His first managerial job was at Dover and after this he was out of the game a while but returned as coach at Wolves in 1953. He later joined Notts County, but after reaching the FA Cup quarter-finals, the side from Meadow Lane were lucky to avoid relegation and after going out in the following season's competition to Rhyl Athletic, he was sacked.

He was not out of work for long and became City's assistant manager to Les McDowall. Later he was promoted as McDowall's successor but could do little to stop the club's slide. After two poor seasons, Poyser resigned as neighbours Manchester United clinched the League Championship.

City's full League record under George Poyser is:

P.	W.	D.	L.	F.	A.
84	34	19	31	147	128

PREMIER LEAGUE

A mediocre finish in the first season of Premier League football, which saw City in 9th place some 27 points behind champions Manchester United, was due largely to an injury crisis. But despite all the doom and gloom, there were some high spots. David White scored 11 goals in the first 15 matches – if he had been able to maintain his phenomenal early season strike-rate, City's season may have turned out differently. Mid-fielder Gary Flitcroft emerged from nowhere as one of the finds of the season.

City's second season in the Premiership will be remembered at Maine Road for the events which took place in the boardroom rather than on the pitch. After the first four games had failed to produce a City victory, Peter Swales brought in journalist John Maddock as general manager and unknown to manager Peter Reid. Within six days, Reid was fired and Oxford manager Brian Horton named as the new boss. It was revealed in the press that former Maine Road favourite Francis Lee was considering trying to take over and so the cry from the terraces was "Swales out, Franny in!"

In November, City led United 2-0 but lost 3-2. Swales decided to step down as chairman and after long negotiations, Lee and his consortium took over. New players arrived to help City's fight against relegation, David Rocastle, Peter Beagrie, Paul Walsh and Uwe Rosler, while last season's top-scorer David White moved on. The new players took time to settle, but three wins and seven draws from their last 12 games ensured safety.

In 1994-95 the die was cast for the Blues on the opening day at Highbury as City went down 3-0 with Kevin Campbell scoring after just two minutes. It was going to be one of the recurring themes

Uwe Rosler, one of the new faces.

Flitcroft in action, 1992.

through City's topsy-turvy campaign. But then Horton's men got themselves up and running with two magnificent home wins, 3-0 v West Ham and 4-0 v Everton. Early October brought one of the games of the season to Maine Road with a six-goal thriller against Nottingham Forest. The Blues then won 2-1 at Loftus Road and followed it up with a 5-2 hammering of Tottenham Hotspur. Faced with their biggest test of the season so far, City were demolished 5-0 as Manchester United ran riot at Maine Road. But the Blues bounced back with three successive victories. A second drubbing by United sent the Blues to their lowest position of the season in the Premiership.

Manager Horton asked for one final effort and the players responded by beating Liverpool at Maine Road, before shocking eventual champions Blackburn Rovers at Ewood Park. Two successive draws ensured City's Premiership safety.

City's full record in the Premier League is:

P.	W.	D.	L.	F.	A.
126	36	43	47	147	164

PROGRAMMES

Manchester City's first match programme was published in September 1898 and was known as "The Official Programme". It was very similar to a weekly magazine and not only contained information about City but about the other Manchester area clubs as well.

In 1900, the title was changed to "The Official" but in 1903 the club began to publish their own programme known as "Blue and White". This title remained until 1954 when it disappeared completely following variations over the years. Over the last thirty years or so, the City programme design has changed almost every season. A 1958 programme is shown overleaf, to contrast with a more recent example of a City v United programme cover.

PROMOTION

City have won promotion on nine occasions, six of them as champions (see earlier entry). When Portsmouth beat the Blues for promotion to the First Division in 1926-27, they did so with the narrowest margin ever to decide a promotion or relegation issue. Portsmouth's average was 1.7755 while City's was 1.7705, a winning margin of five thousandths of a goal.

In 1950-51, City were unbeaten in the first 10 league games of the season, but the last three matches resulted in draws and they finished as runners-up to Preston. In 1984-85 promotion looked a distinct possibility as City beat Wolves 4-0 on 29th December and went on to lose only one of their next ten league games. Promotion would be guaranteed if City could win their last game. This they did thrashing Charlton Athletic 5-1.

In 1988-89 the last few games of the season ended in nail-biting draws and for the last league match of May 1989, City needed just one point for promotion. Bradford City were 1-0 up as the final whistle approached, but City hung on and suddenly Tony Morley found the equaliser. The Blues were going up!

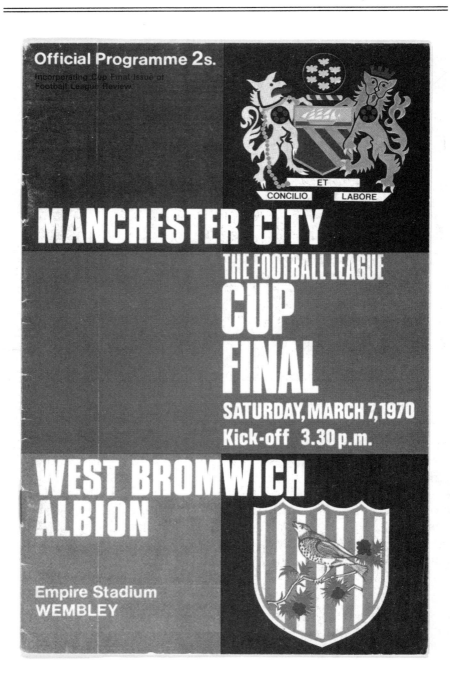

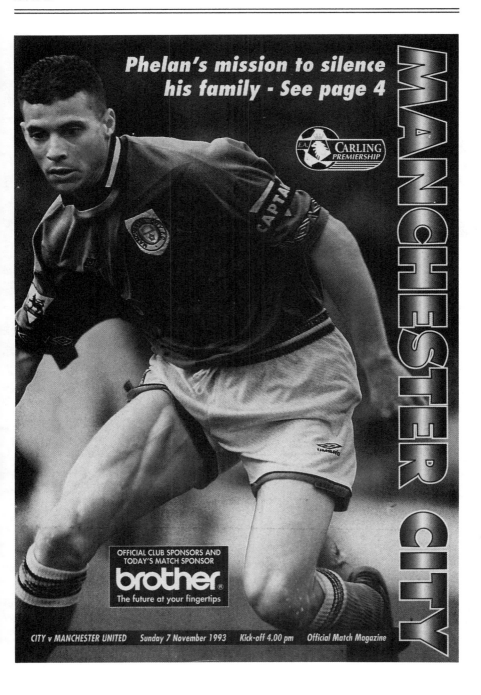

Phelan's mission to silence
his family - See page 4

F.A. CARLING PREMIERSHIP

OFFICIAL CLUB SPONSORS AND
TODAY'S MATCH SPONSOR

brother®
The future at your fingertips

MANCHESTER CITY

CITY v MANCHESTER UNITED   Sunday 7 November 1993   Kick-off 4.00 pm   Official Match Magazine

REID, PETER

Reid in action against Liverpool, 1993.

As a player, Peter Reid had to make a brave recovery from a series of injuries to resurrect his career. Joining Bolton Wanderers as an apprentice, he was a regular in the Trotters' 1977-78 Second Division championship team. In a three-year spell at Burnden Park, he suffered a broken leg and knee cap, torn ligaments and cartilage problems.

He moved to Everton in December 1982 for a bargain £60,000 and was voted PFA Player of the Year in 1985, when the Goodison Park club won the League Championship, European Cup-Winners Cup and reached the FA Cup Final. The following year his inclusion in the England side for the World Cup Finals did a lot to bolster the side.

He joined Manchester City on a free transfer from Queen's Park Rangers in December 1989 and eleven months later following Howard Kendall's departure, he was appointed player-manager. He helped City avoid relegation and continued to play despite the duties of management. He took the club to two excellent seasons in Division One, without winning any trophies. They reached the quarter-finals of the FA Cup but lost to Spurs. Some fans marred a good game by running on the pitch and looking for a confrontation with the opposition supporters. On 26th August 1993, Reid along with his assistant Sam Ellis was sacked on the recommendation of new general manager John Maddock. City's full League record under Peter Reid is:

P.	W.	D.	L.	F.	A.
111	48	27	36	165	139

RELEGATION

Manchester City have on eight occasions experienced the anguish of relegation; less often than many other clubs of a similar age. The first came in 1901-02 but within a season the Blues were back in Division One. City finished in the bottom two in 1908-09 but once again were promoted after just one season in the Second Division.

City were relegated a third time at the end of the 1925-26 season after losing their final game 3-2 at Newcastle, whilst Leeds and Burnley won their games to leap frog over the Blues. Their 89 goals is the most ever scored by a relegated club. Relegation at the end of the 1937-38 season was a great disappointment as the previous season, City had won the League Championship.

In 1949-50 City finished twenty-first out of 22 Division One teams and boasted only one away win in the League, a 2-1 success at Sunderland in April 1950. Relegation in 1962-63 was followed by three seasons in Division Two before promotion and seventeen seasons in the top flight. Finishing twentieth in the First Division in 1982-83, City were relegated for a seventh time. The last time the club were relegated was 1986-87 when City went through the entire season without an away win!

REVIE PLAN

Named after Don Revie one of City's "big money" buys of the early 1950s and later England manager, it involved Revie playing a deep-lying centre-forward role in a manner similar to that which had helped bring success to the brilliant Hungarian team of that era.

ROBERTS, FRANK

When Manchester City signed Frank Roberts from Bolton Wanderers in October 1922 they paid out the considerable sum of £3,400. Though Bolton made quite a profit on the deal, they must have regretted letting the prolific Roberts go. He repaid City with an average of a goal every other game and in 1924-25 he reached the peak of his career as he revelled in the Maine Road mud to score 31 goals in 38 league games that season. It was also the season when he won his first England cap against Belgium and represented the Football League. He went on to win four England caps altogether and played for City in the 1926 FA Cup Final against his former club. He also top scored for City in 1927-28 when they won the Second Division championship, but in June 1929 he was transferred to Manchester Central and later played for Horwich R.M.I.

ROYAL VISITS

City's Hyde Road ground was one of the more important football grounds and welcomed its first royal visitor, King Edward VII around the turn of the century. Royalty also visited the ground in 1920 when King George V watched a game between City and Liverpool on 27th March. The Blues won 2-1.

The Duke of Edinburgh came to Maine Road in May 1964 when City played United in a charity match for the Duke of Edinburgh trophy and also the Manchester Senior Cup.

RUGBY LEAGUE

Maine Road proved to be a versatile arena during the summer of 1947 as the Rugby League Championship play-off between Dewsbury and Wigan was held there on 21st June – the FA Cup semi-final replay between Burnley and Liverpool had been played there as were Manchester United's games following the bomb damage at Old Trafford.

In fact, a total of eleven such Rugby League play-off Finals occurred at Maine Road between 1938 and 1956 with City being absolutely delighted with their share of the gate receipts.

SAUNDERS, RON

A bustling all-action centre-forward, Ron Saunders made his league debut for Everton in 1951, but after only three appearances, he moved to non-league Tonbridge. His league career was resurrected by Gillingham who signed him in May 1957. Portsmouth saw his potential and he went on to make 258 League and cup appearance for Pompey scoring 156 goals before later playing for Watford and Charlton.

Saunders started on the road to management with Southern League Yeovil Town in 1968 but after just twelve months mooed to Oxford United, where he did a remarkably good job in a short period. Obviously impressed, Norwich City offered Saunders their manager's post in July 1969. After taking the Canaries to the Second Division championship in 1971-72 and to the final of the Football League Cup, Saunders resigned after a poor start to the 1973-74 season.

Employed as Manchester City manager in November 1973, he only lasted five months before being sacked, despite taking the club to the League Cup Final, where they lost 2-1 to Wolves. He later managed Aston Villa, Birmingham City and West Bromwich Albion before leaving the game for good.

City's full League record under Ron Saunders is:

P.	W.	D.	L.	F.	A.
25	8	8	9	21	26

SECOND DIVISION

Manchester City have had nine separate spells in the Second Division. They gained admittance to the Second Division of the Football League in 1892. After reaching the promotion-deciding "Test Matches" in 1896, City achieved First Division status after seven years. Following relegation in 1901-02, the Blues bounced back straightaway winning the Second Division championship at the first attempt. likewise in 1909-10, when they were relegated the season before.

Relegated in 1925-26, it took City two seasons this time to return to the top flight, but only because of the narrowest margin ever in a promotion race. Had the issue been on goal difference, City would have been promoted instead of Portsmouth. In 1927-28 there was no mistake whatsoever, as City scored a century of goals to win their fourth Second Division title. The club spent the next ten seasons in the First Division before relegation in 1937-38. It was 1946-47, the first post-war season before City were back in the top flight, but after just three seasons, they were relegated. However, as in 1902-03 and 1909-10, the Blues only needed a season before regaining their place in Division One. Relegated in 1962-63, City spent three seasons in the Second Division before winning the title in 1965-66, a season which saw them undefeated at home. In the eighties, City spent two more spells in the Second Division, each of two seasons each before being promoted to the First Division in 1988-89.

City's all-time record in the Second Division is:

P.	W.	D.	L.	F.	A.
786	402	173	211	1652	1082

SEMI-FINALS

Manchester City have appeared in a total of 14 semi-finals in attempts to get to Wembley with only one game between them and the Twin Towers. On 19th March 1904, City beat Sheffield Wednesday 3-1 with goals from Meredith, Gillespie and Turnbull.

City's 1924 semi-final match against Newcastle United at St Andrew's was Billy Meredith's last game for the club. Sadly it resulted in a 2-0 defeat. The all-Manchester semi-final of the 1925-26 season was played at Bramall Lane where Tommy Browell with a couple of goals and Frank Roberts scored in an impressive 3-0 win for City. City were robbed in 1931-32 when a shot from Arsenal's Cliff Bastin in the last minute took the Gunners to Wembley – all that after the Blues had dominated for most of the play. City were involved in the following years semi-final against Derby County at Huddersfield. The Rams were hot favourites but it was the Blues who made it, with goals from Toseland, Tilson and McMullan in a 3-2 win.

On 17th March 1934, City defeated Aston Villa 6-1 in the semi-final at Huddersfield with four of the goals coming from Fred Tilson. There followed a twenty-one year gap before the Blues next appearance in a semi-final, Roy Clarke scoring the only goal of the game against Sunderland. Twelve months later, City were involved in this stage of the competition again and again won by the score of 1-0 with Bobby Johnstone grabbing the all-important goal.

City's next semi-final was a two-legged Football League Cup affair against Stoke City. After losing 2-0 at the Victoria Ground, a Derek Kevan goal in the second leg wasn't enough to put them in the Final.

In 1968-69 a Tommy Booth goal was enough to give the Blues victory over Everton in the FA Cup semi-final at Villa Park. The following season City played United in the two-legged Football League Cup semi-final. City dominated the first leg at Maine Road and won 2-1 with goals from Bell and Lee, the latter with a late penalty. In the return, United led 2-1 with just minutes remaining but Mike Summerbee equalised to take City through to the final 4-3 on aggregate.

In 1973-74, City played Plymouth Argyle in the League Cup and drew the first leg 1-1 at Home Park. In the return goals from Bell and Lee gave City victory and a place in the Final. City's last appearance in a League Cup semi-final was in 1975-76 against Middlesbrough. After losing 1-0 at Ayresome Park, City bounced back to win the second leg 4-0 with goals from Oakes, Keegan, Barnes and Royle. City's last FA Cup semi-final was in 1981 when it took an extra-time goal from Paul Power to beat Ipswich Town and take them to Wembley.

SHAMROCK TROPHY

On 18th March 1991, Manchester City achieved cup success in the Shamrock Trophy. The Blues drew 2-2 with Shamrock Rovers in Dublin, but won the penalty shoot-out by 4-2. Reserve team 'keeper Martyn Margetson proved his value to the City side when he saved two spot kicks.

SIMOD CUP

The Simod Cup replaced the Full Members' Cup for the 1987-88 season. City's first match that season saw them beat Plymouth Argyle 6-2 with Tony Adcock hitting a hat-trick. In the second round, the Blues went down 2-0 at home to Chelsea. The following season saw City go out of the competition in the opening match, losing 3-2 to Blackburn Rovers at Ewood Park. This being the club's last game in the Simod Cup.

SMITH, GEORGE

Signing for the Blues in 1938, war intervened and after only a handful of games for City in the war league and some guest appearances for Hearts, he went abroad to serve his country in the services. A gunshot wound sustained in South Africa left him with a badly injured hand, but that obviously did not detract from his footballing ability and in 1944 he returned to play for City in the wartime league, scoring a hat-trick against Tranmere in his first match. The following season he scored all four goals in the wartime league match against Manchester United, as the Reds were beaten 4-1.

He made his Football League debut for the Maine Road side on 31st August 1946 when the Blues took on Leicester City. On 14th June 1947 City completed their final game of an extended season against an already-relegated Newport County. George Smith scored all five City goals in a 5-1 win to equal a club individual record. That season City won the Second Division championship and Smith missed only four league games as he top-scored with 23 goals.

After 179 first-team appearances and 80 goals, he was transferred to Chesterfield for £5,000 and enjoyed some good years at Saltergate.

SPONSORS

City's first sponsors were Saab who sponsored the club from 1982 to 1984. They were followed by Phillips until 1987, when the club's current sponsors, Brother, took over.

SUBSTITUTES

Substitutes were first allowed in the Football League in the 1965-66 season. The first appearance of a substitute in league football came down the road at Burnden Park when Charlton Athletic's Keith Peacock came on during Wanderers' 4-2 win. Manchester City's first substitute was Roy Cheetham who came on for Mike Summerbee in the club's fourth game of the season, a 4-2 win at Wolverhampton.

The first goal-scoring number twelve was Matt Gray who scored for City in their 4-3 defeat at Cardiff City on 18th September 1965.

The greatest number of substitutes used in a single season by City under the single substitute rule was twenty-six in 1984-85, but since 1986-87 two substitutes have been allowed and in both 1989-90 and 1991-92, the club used fifty-one.

The greatest number of substitute appearances for City has been made by Clive Allen, who came on during twenty-two league games before his move to Chelsea. It was in 1989-90 that Ian Brightwell caused the City records on the matter of substitutes to be rewritten, with an extraordinary fourteen league appearances in the number twelve shirt.

SUMMERBEE, MIKE

Mike Summerbee was a West Country boy from a footballing family, his uncle George having been a professional with Chester, Preston and Barrow. When Mike left school, he played for his home town club

Mike Summerbee, 1971

Cheltenham, until Swindon Town spotted his potential. He played more than 200 games for Swindon, helping them clinch promotion from Division Three in 1963.

Inevitably, his dashing excursions along the wings caught the eye of some of the bigger clubs and in August 1965, this tenacious winger became the first of Joe Mercer's signings when City paid £30,000 to sign him. He joined City at the time when England manager Alf Ramsey was beginning to dispense with wingers on the international scene, but he quickly adapted to the demands being made on the new breed of midfield wide men.

In his first season he helped City to win the Second Division title and then in a three-year spell between 1968 and 1970 – the most successful period in the club's history – he played a significant role in City's triumphs.

Though he wasn't a prolific goal-scorer, he did hit a hat-trick as City beat Reading 7-0 at Elm Park in an FA Cup third round replay after a goal-less draw at Maine Road. Primarily right-footed, he made an immediate impression at Maine Road with his diligence and industry. He tackled back and shouldered his share of the defensive duties – he was a hard, uncompromising player. In the FA Cup Final of 1969, it was Summerbee who went down the right wing avoiding the challenges of Nish and Woollett to cut the ball back from the dead-ball line for Neil Young to strike home the only goal of the game. Manchester City's attacking power was their strength at the time of the Mercer-Allison partnership and Summerbee's forays on the right were supported by the running of the more orthodox Tony Coleman on the left to give City a compelling urgency that few other First Division teams could match.

He certainly enjoyed the limelight. A confident player on the field, deputising as a central striker when they had injuries, he was a fashionable dresser off it and part-owner of a boutique with United's George Best. He won eight full England caps, making his debut against Scotland in 1968. He spent ten years with Manchester City before he moved to Turf Moor in 1975 for a fee of £25,000. His career later took him to Blackpool, followed by a spell as player-manager at Stockport County. A good skilful player, Mike Summerbee was the working man's winger.

SUNDAY FOOTBALL

The first ever Sunday matches in the Football League took place on 20th January 1974 during the three-day week imposed by the government during its trial of strength with the coal-miners. City had to wait until the following Sunday, 27th January before playing their first game on the Sabbath, losing 4-1 against Notts County at Meadow Lane – Frank Carrodus scoring for City.

The club's next Sunday game was the Full Members' Cup Final at Wembley against Chelsea on 23rd March 1986; City losing 5-4 in a thrilling game.

Since then, the club have played numerous League and Cup games on a Sunday, notably at home to Tottenham Hotspur on 7th March 1993, when not only did City lose 4-2, but there was a pitch invasion during the game.

SUSTAINED SCORING

During the early games of the 1924-25 season, Frank Roberts scored two goals in each of the games against Bury, Liverpool, Newcastle United and West Ham and put one away against Nottingham Forest. He also hit a hat-trick in the game against Sheffield United, the seventh match of the season to make it 12 goals in the first eight games of the campaign.

In 1957-58, Irish centre-forward Billy McAdams scored eleven goals in ten consecutive league games, plus another goal in a friendly.

SWIFT, FRANK

Frank Swift set the standards for goalkeepers before and after the Second World War. Joining Manchester City from Fleetwood on 21st October 1932, he made his league debut on Christmas Day the following year against Derby County.

Beginning with his first full season in the league side, Frank Swift was ever-present for four consecutive seasons and missed only one game in 1938-39.

In 1934 he was a member of the successful City side that lifted the FA Cup when they beat Portsmouth 2-1. At half-time, Pomey led 1-0 with Swift conceding that he might have saved the goal had he been wearing gloves! Fred Tilson hit two second-half goals and on the final whistle, the 19-year-old Swift turned to collect his cap and gloves and fainted! Afterwards he said "Fancy a great strapping fellow like me fainting in front of all these people and the King. "

Swifty could fool around with the best of them. He often used to make an acrobatic flying dive that would have the crowd roaring even though he knew the ball was going well wide.

In 1935, he made an appearance for The Rest in a trial match against England, but it was to be after the war when he played in a full international. He won 19 caps for England, his first against Northern Ireland in 1946 and played in many wartime internationals as well as gaining First and Second Division championship medals along with that 1934 FA Cup-Winners' medal.

He had been skipper of Manchester City for a couple of seasons, when against Italy in 1948, he became the first goalkeeper to captain England. He had a magnificent game, one save from Gabetto the centre-forward, was out of this world, leaving the Italian beating the turf with his fists.

Frank Swift had enormous hands, with a finger span of almost a foot; he would catch the ball in one hand and then hold it over the centre-forward's head just out of reach – he was loved by the crowd. A spectacular goalkeeper, he was daring and sometimes even headed shots away. He was one of the first goalkeepers to elect to throw the ball to a colleague rather than opt for the usual long kick down the field, most used in those days. An excellent shot-stopper, he was a great personality both on and off the field.

Although he retired in September 1949, his registration was held by City until May 1955.

Frank Swift was tragically killed in the Munich Air Disaster of 1958 when accompanying Manchester United as a newspaper reporter.

TELEVISION

The first City league game to be televised live was the match at Maine Road against Chelsea on 4th May 1984. Unfortunately, the Blues lost 2-0.

Frank Swift

TENNENT-CALEDONIAN CUP

In August 1976, City took part in a four-club tournament in Scotland. Their first match was against Southampton, a Dennis Tueart goal giving them a 1-1 draw. There then followed a penalty shoot-out but after each side had scored 11 penalties, Southampton went through to the final on the toss of a coin! In the play-off for third place, City beat Partick Thistle 4-1.

TEST MATCHES

When the 1895-96 season ended, the top of the Second Division table read:

	P.	W.	D.	L.	F.	A.	Pts
Liverpool	30	22	2	6	106	32	46
Manchester City	30	21	4	5	63	38	46

In those days it was customary for the bottom two clubs of the First Division and the top two of the Second Division to play 'Test Matches' to decide which two should be numbered among the sixteen clubs of the First Division. There was no automatic promotion and relegation as we know it today.

In April 1896 City's results were:

April 18th	West Bromwich Albion	Home	Drew	1-1
April 20th	West Bromwich Albion	Away	Lost	1-6
April 25th	Small Heath	Home	Won	3-0
April 27th	Small Heath	Away	Lost	0-8

City were robbed of promotion by the 8-0 defeat even though the club had lost only five league matches while in the Second Division, which gave them second place.

TEXACO CUP

The predecessor of the Anglo-Scottish Cup, it was launched in 1970-71 and was for English, Irish and Scottish club sides not involved in European competitions that season.

City's first match in the competition was at home to Airdrieonians on 15th September 1971. Goals from Mellor and Doyle gave them a 2-2 draw but they went down 2-0 in the second leg at Broomfield Park where they had their appearance money with-held for fielding a weak eleven.

In August 1974, City played three Group One matches all away from Maine Road. They drew 1-1 at Blackpool, lost 4-2 at Sheffield United and though they won 2-1 at Oldham, they failed to qualify.

THOMSON, JOCK

A well-built wing-half who played a powerful and commanding game, Jock Thomson won two First Division and one Second Division championship winners' medals and an FA Cup winners' medal with Everton. He gained his only cap for Scotland against Wales at Tynecastle in October 1932 and had an amazing first two years at Goodison Park, experiencing relegation, followed by winning the Second Division and the First Division championships. He won his FA Cup medal in 1933 when Everton beat Manchester City 3-0.

Appointed City manager in July 1947, he did not have a happy time at Maine Road. City finished seventh in 1948-49 but were relegated to Division Two the following season and Thomson left the club.

City's full League record under Jock Thomson is:

P.	W.	D.	L.	F.	A.
126	38	40	48	135	166

THORNLEY, IRVINE

A butcher by trade, Irvine Thornley joined Manchester City from Glossop, his home town club in April 1904 for £800, although the FA later discovered some "irregularities" concerning his transfer.

Thornley was something of a controversial player who had one or two brushes with authority. In January 1912 when captaining City, shortly after returning to the side following an eye injury, he was sent off at Aston Villa! Despite this side to his character, he was such a popular figure at Hyde Road that he was the first player to receive £1,000 for his benefit.

A wholehearted and tireless player, Thornley scored 92 league goals for City in 195 appearances. He was capped by England against Wales in March 1907 and played for the Football League on two occasions, against the Irish and Scottish Leagues.

He won a Second Division championship medal with City in 1909-10 before joining South Shields in August 1912. He scored over 60 goals for the Tyneside club before ending his career in the Scottish League with Hamilton Academicals.

TILSON, FRED

Despite his career at Maine Road being frequently dogged by injury, Fred Tilson made a great contribution to the City side of the 1930s.

He arrived at Maine Road on a double transfer with Eric Brook from Barnsley. Although small in stature for a centre-forward, Tilson was a goal-scoring genius and on 26th November 1932 scored four goals against Aston Villa in City's 5-2 win. That season, he was injured in a league game shortly before the FA Cup Final and missed the Wembley game. He was determined to make amends the following season and put another four goals past Aston Villa in the semi-final of the FA Cup as City returned to Wembley. He scored both City's goals in the final as the Blues secured the trophy for the first time since 1904.

That summer he won the first of four England caps (scoring six goals) and in 1936-37 he was instrumental in bringing the League Championship to Maine Road. Although absent with injury for almost half the league games, he scored 15 goals in the 23 games he did play in, including a marvellous hat-trick against Derby County at the Baseball Ground.

After leaving City in November 1938, he had spells at Northampton and York City before returning to Maine Road to work as coach, assistant-manager and chief scout respectively.

TOSELAND, ERNIE

Ernie Toseland was a flying winger who began his career with

Coventry City, for whom he scored 11 goals in only 22 games. It was this form that went a long way to persuading Manchester City to sign him in March 1929. He made his debut for City against Bury the following month and supplied the crosses for Johnson and Tilson to score. Toseland opened his account in the next game as City beat Aston Villa 3-0.

Over the next ten seasons, Ernie Toseland hardly missed a game. He won a League Championship medal and an FA Cup winners' medal but his only representative honour was an appearance for the Football League against the Irish League in September 1929. There were many who expressed their surprise that Ernie Toseland never won an England cap, but there were many fine wingers on the scene in the 1930s.

After 409 first-team appearances and 75 goals he moved to Hillsborough but managed only 15 appearances for the Owls before the hostilities curtailed the League. He returned to Maine Road to guest for City and as late as 1945-46 was still playing in the Cheshire County League.

TRANSFERS

The transfer of players has always been a feature of football though in the early days some unusual arrangements were often made.

City created a British record of £450 when Johnny McMahon came from Preston in 1902 and the following year equalled the record with the signing of winger George Dorsett from West Bromwich Albion. Two years later, Irvine Thornley almost became the first player to cost the club £1,000. City paid Glossop £450 but infringements of the rules cost them a fine of £250 by the FA, an alleged bribe of £150 went astray, there was a signing-on fee and some advanced wages – the whole amount was a few pounds short of four figures!

Bert Sproston was chosen at right-back for Tottenham Hotspur v Manchester City in a Division Two match at Maine Road on 5th November 1938 and his name was printed on the match programme. But he was then transferred to City and turned out for them against Spurs on the day of the game – City won 2-0.

Since the war, the size of transfer fees escalated incredibly. When

manager Les McDowall signed Denis Law from Huddersfield Town
in 1961, a new British transfer fee of £55,000 was created. Steve Daley
was the first player to arrive at Maine Road who cost over £1 million
when he signed from Wolves in September 1979.

The club's most expensive signings are the former Wimbledon pair
of Keith Curle and Terry Phelan, each of whom cost £2.5 million!

TRAUTMANN, BERT

Arriving in England in April 1945, it was at a Prisoner of War camp
at Ashton-in-Makerfield that Bert Trautmann first tried his hand at
goalkeeping.

He said later that it was his training as a German paratrooper that
helped him cushion the ball as he fell. At the end of the Second World
War, he was released from the Prisoner of War camp and went to work
on a farm and began to play for St Helens Town. After some impressive displays, he signed for City on 2nd November 1949. Seventeen
days later, he made his first-team debut for City against Bolton
Wanderers.

Of course, replacing the great and very popular Frank Swift,
Trautmann came in for a great deal of hostility from the Maine Road
supporters. This perhaps was not surprising, for the war was still
fresh in the minds of many people and as an ex-German paratrooper
and Prisoner of War, he could hardly have expected the warmest of
Lancashire welcomes. later marrying the City club secretary's daugh-
ter, he soon won over the hearts of the Maine Road followers.

Trautmann was a member of the victorious City side of 1956 that
lifted the FA Cup beating Birmingham City 3-1 at Wembley. With just
fifteen minutes remaining, Bert Trautmann dived at the feet of Peter
Murphy, the Birmingham inside-forward and was caught in the neck
by his knee. After receiving lengthy treatment, the goalkeeper continued courageously, though he was obviously in great pain. It was
only after the match had finished that it was discovered that he had
played the closing minutes with a broken neck. He missed the chance
to play for his native Germany, being out of the game for the next
seven months.

Bert Trautmann, diving at an attacker's feet

There is no doubt though, if he'd been born in this country, he would have gone on to play for England.

Besides his two appearances for City in FA Cup Finals at Wembley he was voted the 1956 Footballer of the Year. He also had to overcome personal tragedy that same year, when his five-year-old son was killed in a road accident.

He retired on 10th May 1964 after playing in over 500 games for City. He later played for non-league Wellington Town and then became general manager of Stockport County, before going abroad to coach.

TUEART, DENNIS

Moving to Manchester City from Sunderland, Dennis Tueart will long be remembered for his spectacular goal for the Blues against Newcastle United in the 1976 Football League Cup Final at Wembley. With his back to the goal, Tueart hooked the ball over his right shoulder to leave 'keeper Mahoney rooted to the spot and restore City's lead and leave the Magpies a beaten side.

Dennis Tueart, 1982

He had been in the Sunderland side which caused a shock by winning the FA Cup in 1973. A former Newcastle Boys player, Tueart joined City from the Roker Park club for £275,000 in March 1974 and made his debut in the Manchester derby that month.

While at Maine Road, Tueart gained six England caps. He took time out to play for the renowned New York Cosmos club between 1978 and 1980 before returning to Manchester. City sold him to the NASL club for £250,000 and bought him back for £150,000. Tueart won a League Cup winners' medal with City in 1976 and played in the 1981 FA Cup Final. One of the finest forwards of his era, exciting crowds wherever he played, he left City on a free transfer for Stoke City in July 1983.

UEFA CUP

Formerly known as the Fairs Cup, its name was changed in 1971 when it became the UEFA Cup.

City first participated in the competition in 1972-73, but their stay was short-lived as they went out 4-3 on aggregate to Spanish club Valencia in the first round. The club fared no better in 1976-77 going down 2-1 on aggregate to the Italian giants Juventus, again in the opening round. The following season City had another crack at this competition, but were forced out by the Polish side Widzew Lodz. The Blues went out on the away goals rule, having drawn 2-2 at Maine Road in the first-leg and 0-0 in Poland.

In 1978-79 City at last progressed past the first round beating Dutch side Twente Enschede 4-3 on aggregate. In round two, the Blues opponents were Standard Liege. Brian Kidd scored two goals and Palmer and Hartford one apiece as City won 4-0. However, they lost the return 2-0 and were indebted to Joe Corrigan who kept them in the game with some fine saves. A 5-2 aggregate victory over A.C. Milan took the club into the quarter-final, where they faced Borussia Monchengladbach. But after drawing 1-1 at home, the Blues went down 3-1 in the second leg in Germany.

UNDEFEATED

Manchester City have remained undefeated at home throughout four league seasons: 1895-96; 1904-05; 1920-21 and 1965-66.

The club's best and longest undefeated home sequence in the Football League is of forty-one matches between 25th December 1919 and 3rd December 1921.

City's longest run of undefeated Football League matches, home and away is twenty-two – a total achieved on two occasions – between 26th December 1936 and 1st May 1937 and from 16th November 1946 to 19th April 1947.

UTILITY PLAYERS

A utility player is one of those particularly gifted footballers who can play in several or even many different positions. Tom Holford was probably Manchester City's earliest utility player. He played in every position except goalkeeper, though with City he played mainly at half-back. Jimmy Meadows played in seven different positions for the Blues before being capped for England at right-back.

After about the mid-1960s, players were encouraged to become more adaptable and to see their roles as less stereotyped. At the same time, however, much less attention came to be paid to the implication of wearing a certain numbered shirt and accordingly, some of the more versatile players came to wear almost all the different numbered shirts at some stage or another, although this did not necessarily indicate a vast variety of positions. David Connor spent ten years at Maine Road and though he only made 130 league appearances, he was something of a utility player, serving City in every first-team position except goalkeeper and centre-half. Glyn Pardoe was City's youngest ever league debutante and like Connor, he too went on to play in every position except goalkeeper and centre-half. Ian Brightwell is a versatile player who scored important goals in the club's 1988-89 promotion season. He has worn every outfield shirt and only needs to don the goalkeepers top to have worn a full set. Paul Lake is without doubt Manchester City's most versatile player of recent years. He has appeared as a full-back, central defender, midfield player and an out-and-out striker.

VICTORIES

In a Season:

City's greatest number of victories in a season is twenty-six achieved in seasons 1946-47 when the club won the Second Division championship and 1967-68 when the Blues topped the First Division.

In a Match:

City's best victories in the major competitions are as follows:

Home:

Football League	11-3	v	Lincoln City	1894-95
FA Cup	11-4	v	Crystal Palace	1925-26
F.Lg. Cup	6-0	v	Scunthorpe United	1974-75
	6-0	v	Torquay United	1983-84

Away:

Football League	9-3	v	Tranmere Rovers	1938-39
FA Cup	7-0	v	Reading	1967-68
F.Lg. Cup	6-3	v	Plymouth Argyle	1988-89

These results are for matches played since the Club's admission to the Football League, though prior to that when City were known as Ardwick they beat Liverpool Stanley 12-0 in a qualifying round of the FA Cup on 4th October 1890.

WARTIME

First World War:

In spite of the outbreak of war in 1914, the major football leagues embarked upon their planned programme of matches for the ensuing season and these were completed on schedule at the end of April the following The season saw the club finish fifth in the First Division.

During the First World War, the full league programme was suspended and City took part in the regional competition. They finished first in 1915-16 and were never out of the top five during each season of the war. Horace Barnes scored 56 goals in 57 regional league games for City.

Second World War:

In contrast to the events of 1914, once war was declared on 3rd September 1939 the Football League programme of 1939-40 was immediately suspended and the government forbade any major sporting events, so that for a while there was no football of any description.

City had opened the season with a 4-3 reversal at Leicester, following it with a 1-1 draw at home to Bury. On 2nd September they beat

Chesterfield 2-0 with both goals scored by Jack Milsom. On 21st October 1939, City in common with other league clubs, began regional competitive football. They suffered some embarrassing defeats. In January 1944 they lost 7-1 to Bury and by the same score to Chester eleven months later.

During the war years, Blues fans were able to see both Manchester clubs at the Maine Road ground as United's Old Trafford had been severely damaged by bombs in 1941.

WEATHER CONDITIONS

On Saturday 1st September 1906, Manchester City finished their Division One home game against Arsenal with just six men; the other five had gone off with heat exhaustion. City lost the game 4-1 on what is thought to be the hottest day a League programme has ever been completed – the temperature was over 90°F (32°C).

WILD, WILF

Wilf Wild worked for Manchester City for 30 years as assistant-secretary and secretary-manager. When he was in charge of teams affairs, he took the club to a League title and two FA Cup Finals and was also in control throughout the war years.

Many fine players arrived at Maine Road during Wild's period in control. They included Peter Doherty, whom he bought for £10,000 and Alex Herd, Sam Barkas and Frank Swift. City reached the 1933 FA Cup Final but lost 3-0 to Everton. The following year, City returned to Wembley and this time won the FA Cup, beating Portsmouth 2-1. When City won the League Championship in 1936-37, their success came in remarkable fashion. At Christmas, they had only 20 points from 20 games but in the last 22 games they won 15 and drew the other seven to take the title. Incredibly, City were relegated the following season despite scoring more goals than anybody else in the First Division.

Like Ernest Mangnall before him, he had to guide City through a world war. He was still in charge when peacetime football resumed in 1946, but in November of that year he reverted to secretarial duties and was replaced by Sam Cowan. He was still in office when he died in December 1950. His wife Betty worked in the club's main office up until the early 1960s.

City's full League record under Wilf Wild is:

P.	W.	D.	L.	F.	A.
307	133	64	110	595	495

WORST START

The club's worst ever start to a season was in 1980-81. It took 13 League games to record the first victory of the season, drawing 4 and losing 8 of the opening fixtures. The run ended with a 3-1 success over Tottenham Hotspur at Maine Road on 22nd October 1980.

John Bond replaced Malcolm Allison and between 15th November and January 17th, the Blues lost only one of 10 League matches and finished the season in twelfth position.

XMAS DAY

There was a time when football was regularly played on Christmas Day but in recent years the footballing authorities have dropped the fixture from their calendar. The last time Manchester City played on a Christmas Day was in 1957 when they lost to Burnley 2-1 at Turf Moor. One of the most memorable games played on Christmas Day occurred in 1925 when City went to Gigg Lane and lost 6-5 in an eleven-goal thriller.

After the Christmas Day game at Maine Road in 1946 both teams left the pitch to head for railway station in order to get to the venue of the Boxing Day reverse fixture – down at Home Park, Plymouth!

YOUNG, NEIL

One of Manchester City's first-ever apprentice professionals, Neil

Neil Young, 1967

Young signed for City in the close season of 1960. He made his League debut in November 1961 at Villa Park and though the Blues lost, he had the satisfaction of setting up Peter Dobing for the City goal. His first goal for the club came in his fifth game in a 3-0 win over Ipswich Town. In these early days he was being switched around the forward line, but when Mercer and Allison moved him permanently to the number ten spot, he flourished. They gave him a free-roving commission and he repaid their faith in him by scoring 17 League and Cup goals to end up leading goal-scorer. He was top scorer in City's championship season of 1967-68 and crowned a great season by scoring twice in City's 4-3 win at Newcastle.

It was Neil Young's splendid left-foot shot that won the Blues the FA Cup in 1969 when Leicester's Peter Shilton was left groping fresh air. The following year he scored one of City's two goals in Vienna which brought victory over Gornik Zabrze in the European Cup-Winners' Cup. His only representative honour was in the England Youth team and it was surprising that he was not considered at Under-23 or full level.

In January 1972, Young moved to Preston North End for £48,000 and later had a short spell with Rochdale before retiring.

A player who always seemed to have something to spare, he is best remembered fondly for his excellent ball control and shooting power, which helped to bring so much success to Maine Road.

Niall Quinn in action against Liverpool, August 1991.

YOUTH CUP

Manchester City carried off the FA Youth Cup for the first and only time in their history in 1986. Their opponents in the final were neighbours and rivals Manchester United. City won the second leg 2-0 at Maine Road after drawing 1-1 at Old Trafford.

City have appeared in two other Finals, losing 2-0 on aggregate to Millwall in 1979 and 3-2 to Aston Villa in 1980.

City's first-ever opponents in the Youth Cup were Bolton Wanderers, whilst the club's best-ever win in the competition is 10-1 at Billingham.

City's Darren Beckford scored hat-tricks in each of the first three rounds of the 1984-85 FA Youth Cup.

ZENITH DATA SYSTEMS CUP

The Zenith Data Systems Cup replaced the Simod Cup for the 1989-90 season. City's first round match in 1990-91 saw them defeat Middlesbrough 2-1 with goals from White and Quinn. In round two, the Blues travelled to Bramall Lane. Two goals from City winger Mark Ward were enough to beat Sheffield United 2-0. In the third round, City again travelled to Yorkshire, but this time they went down 2-0 to Leeds United.

The following season, City travelled to Hillsborough, where they went down 3-2 to Sheffield Wednesday with Colin Hendry grabbing both City goals.

Index

MORE ABOUT THE MANCHESTER FOOTBALL SCENE!

MANCHESTER CITY: MOMENTS TO REMEMBER – John Creighton (£9.95)

Still the definitive account of MCFC's ups and downs, their triumphs and disasters. Fully illustrated with modern and archive action shots.

RED FEVER! FROM MANCHESTER TO RIO AS UNITED SUPPORTERS – Steve Donoghue (£7.95)

A hilarious account of a United fan who travelled the world to support his team. See United through the eyes of a true Red!

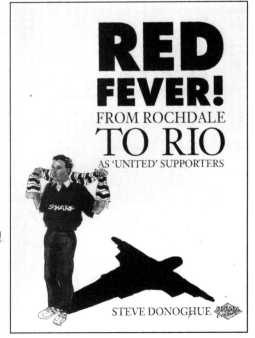

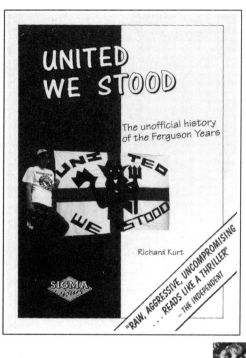

UNITED WE STOOD: the unofficial history of the Ferguson years – Richard Kurt (£6.95)

Here are two books they'd rather you didn't read – both by best-selling author and fanzine writer, Richard Kurt. If easily offended by cutting remarks about the opposition, unkind (but hilarious) cartoons and colourful language, don't buy either of them. But if you want entertainment and incisive analysis, open your wallets now!

DESPATCHES FROM OLD TRAFFORD – Richard Kurt (£6.95)